THE HAUNTED CASTLES OF ENGLAND

For Tammy

THE HAUNTED CASTLES OF ENGLAND

NEIL R. STOREY

PEN & SWORD HISTORY
AN IMPRINT OF PEN & SWORD BOOKS LTD.
YORKSHIRE – PHILADELPHIA

First published in Great Britain in 2026 by
PEN AND SWORD HISTORY
An imprint of
Pen & Sword Books Ltd
Yorkshire – Philadelphia

ISBN 978 1 03618 013 3

A CIP catalogue record for this book is available from the British Library.

Typeset in Times New Roman 11.5/14 by
SJmagic DESIGN SERVICES, India.
Printed and bound in the UK by CPI Group (UK) Ltd.

The Publisher's authorised representative in the EU for product safety is Authorised Rep Compliance Ltd., Ground Floor, 71 Lower Baggot Street, Dublin D02 P593, Ireland.
www.arccompliance.com

For a complete list of Pen & Sword titles please contact
PEN & SWORD BOOKS LIMITED
George House, Units 12 & 13, Beevor Street, Off Pontefract Road,
Barnsley, South Yorkshire, S71 1HN, England
E-mail: enquiries@pen-and-sword.co.uk
Website: www.pen-and-sword.co.uk

or

PEN AND SWORD BOOKS
1950 Lawrence Rd, Havertown, PA 19083, USA
E-mail: uspen-and-sword@casematepublishers.com
Website: www.penandswordbooks.com

MIX
Paper | Supporting responsible forestry
FSC® C013604
FSC www.fsc.org

Contents

Introduction

This royal throne of kings, this scepter'd isle,
This earth of majesty, this seat of Mars,
This other Eden, demi-paradise,
This fortress built by Nature for herself
Against infection and the hand of war,
This happy breed of men, this little world,
This precious stone set in the silver sea,
Which serves it in the office of a wall,
Or as a moat defensive to a house,
Against the envy of less happier lands,
This blessed plot, this earth, this realm, this England.

Shakespeare

It has been said that an Englishman's home is his castle and although most of us today do not live in a castle, there is still a feeling deep inside us that our homes are still our fortresses, our safe spaces to live in. We don't need to assume a sense of grandeur to visit a castle; there are still plenty of these around for us to see, some in superb states of repair, some reduced to ivy-clad ruins, but every one of them will have been a home. Of the many stories a castle has to tell from down the centuries, there will usually be at least one tale that resonates with a visitor.

Most of England's castles, historic buildings and ancient monuments are the backdrop for mysterious tales of paranormal activity. To be honest, there are few buildings that have been around for centuries that have not been the scene of conflict, treachery, crime, persecution, plague and death – tragic, accidental or murderous. Any and every one of these dramatic incidents *could* potentially leave some trace of it in the form of a haunting.

As a boy, I was fortunate to have a mother who loved ghost stories and whenever we went to a castle, she would have found or knew of a spooky story associated with it – the sort of tale that captured my imagination, perhaps even gave me a little shiver but never caused a nightmare. When I got a little older, we looked through ghost books together and planned trips out in the summer holidays to include a castle or ruins, specifically because they were said to be haunted.

I was absolutely fascinated by the subject, but I must admit I was a bit scared by some of the photos which were believed to have captured spirits in the Usborne *World of the Unknown* volume on *Ghosts.* They certainly got my imagination racing. The copy of Hippisley Coxe's *Haunted Britain* is probably the most travelled volume on all my shelves. *The World's Greatest Ghosts* by Nigel Blundell and Roger Boar and the Shire Guide, *Discovering Ghosts* by Leon Metcalfe, were two of my most-read books as a teenager. I love the fact that when I look back through my ghost books that my copy of *The Ghost Hunter's Road Book* by John Harries was awarded to me as a school prize. My headmaster knew me well.

That said, I never dreamed my work as a historian would take me to quite so many haunted places. I have been very fortunate over the years to have had the chance to lead and work on history projects, filming, special events and paranormal investigations with teams from both sides of the Atlantic. During which I have stayed overnight and in some cases over several nights at some of the most haunted castles and historic sites all over the British Isles. Some of them were places I had read about as a boy, shuddered at the stories and never dreamed I would visit them, let alone stay in them for real.

Some castles have an atmosphere that oozes history and a sense of place from the moment you enter them. Some seem like there is little or no atmosphere about the place in daylight when there are members of public around – until dusk falls, then, after all the visitors have gone home and it gets dark and late and oh, my word, what a difference that can make. There are only a few castles where I really do not relish a return visit because of their dark and forbidding atmospheres.

Some are in England and are mentioned in this book, but I shall leave you to visit them and decide for yourself.

I have often been asked if I have seen a ghost. I believe that I have, and I have witnessed all manner of paranormal activity but unless I am confident that I am talking to someone who has had a similar experience, I normally answer that I have seen things that I cannot explain. The truth is, as John Harries pointed out in his introduction to *The Ghost Hunter's Road Book*: 'Ghosts are not unlike the weirder and rarer of the animal and reptilian species. Until one has seen them it is difficult to believe they exist.'

Tales of ghosts, witches, curses, demons, devil dogs, vampires, harbingers of doom and many other creatures of the night have been woven into the fabric of English folklore for centuries. They have made their mark on our culture and historical places, in stories and legends that have been passed down from generation to generation. In this book I do not attempt to prove or disprove the existence of ghosts, nor do I pretend it is encyclopaedic. What I set out to do is share some of my favourite ghost stories, some well known, some infamous in their day and some pretty much forgotten, from royal castles and the Tower of London to castles over the length and breadth of England, from the fortifications of the windswept borderlands in the north to the strongholds of the turbulent midlands, to the bastions of southern England and the Channel coast, to the ancient castles of the eastern counties.

Being known as a historian who finds the history behind the ghost stories, I have set out to uncover the earliest first-hand or published accounts of the hauntings and reproduce them exactly as they appeared; some are from many years ago, but there are also far more recent accounts of ghosts and paranormal activity experienced in and around those ancient walls. I have also tracked down wonderful old photographs of some of the castles in this book that date from the 'golden age' of ghost stories when many of the tales were first published in the late nineteenth and early twentieth centuries, to set the mood for the tales that accompany them.

Over the years I have travelled thousands of miles around Britain in the pursuit of the strange, mysterious and paranormal. I have been to some amazing places, met some great people, enjoyed some wonderful food and drink and have seen some truly beautiful countryside of this enchanted land along the way. Come and join me on this haunted journey … if you dare.

Neil R. Storey
Norwich, 2026

Note: Most of the castles in this book are accessible but some are only open to the public at certain times of the year, so if you are a planning a visit check online to ensure they will be open. Some are private homes, so please be respectful of that and just enjoy the stories.

Chapter 1

The North West

There she sees a damsel bright,
Drest in a silken robe of white,
That shadowy in the moonlight shone
The neck that made that white robe wan.
Samuel Taylor Coleridge

Askerton Castle, Askerton, Cumbria

Built as an unfortified manor house around 1290 as a home for the de Multon family in the heart of Reiver territory, Margaret de Multon, the last of the line, daughter and heiress of Thomas de Multon, was made a ward of Edward II after the death of her father. In around the 1315 Margaret was in the care of Thomas de Beauchamp at Warwick Castle where she eloped by night with Ranulph de Dacre. Dacre was granted a pardon by the king 'for stealing [Margaret] awai in the nighte out of the king's custody' in October 1317 and they married. Whether it was truly a marriage for love or a snatch-and-grab union bringing control of the de Multon lands into the Dacre estates, we shall probably never know. It appears a contract had been made years before with the de Clifford family for Margaret to marry one of their sons when she came of age, but the Dacres and Cliffords came to an arrangement. Still, it does appear like Margaret was treated as a commodity and did not seem to have had much say in the matter.

What is known is the Dacre, Neville and Percy families were some of the oldest established and most powerful on the northern border of England. The Dacre family had proved themselves fighting off Scottish raiders and avenging their depredations. Dacre would go on to earn further laurels leading the English soldiery to victory and sending the Scots to flight at the Battle of Dornock on 25 March 1333. Margaret bore Dacre four sons who would carry on the name and inherit the title in due course. She died in 1361 over forty years after the elopement (or abduction).

One of their descendants was Thomas, Lord Dacre, Lord Warden of the West March who, no doubt mindful of the persistent incursions by the Scots his family had fought for hundreds of years, added crenellated towers to the original range at Askerton in the 1590s, not only enlarging the property but adding to its defences. The castle was renovated by architect Anthony Salvin in the mid-nineteenth century; it is now part of an organic farm, and is not open to the public, but it is the roads around about where the haunting occurs.

The ghost, according to local legend, is named May Marye. She is said, like Margaret, to have been abducted by her lover, flung onto his horse and made off with but there the similarity ends. In this story May Marye was murdered by her lover and her ghost has returned to seek revenge by jumping on the backs of horses passing along the roads near the castle and terrorising those mounted upon them. One story tells of how she conversed with a rider but made him swear on his life that he would never reveal to anyone what they had discussed.

Carlisle Castle, Carlisle, Cumbria

Carlisle Castle began as a Norman-style motte-and-bailey castle built on the orders of William II in 1092 when Cumberland was still considered a part of Scotland. The fortress was well sited as it would be built on the site of the old Roman fort of Luguvalium. Rebuilt as a stone fortress with towers under the orders of Henry I in 1122, the castle is now over 930 years old. It stood on the border of the land of the Reivers and England, and during the conflicts over the centuries it changed hands many times and can rightly claim to be one of the most besieged castles in England.

Falling into disuse, parts of the castle were demolished in the nineteenth century to create raw materials for use locally and make space to create a parade square. The rest of the castle, pretty much what is seen today, was used as a barracks, The castle was Depot of the Border

Regiment from 1881 until 1959, when the regiment amalgamated with the King's Own Royal Regiment (Lancaster) to form the King's Own Royal Border Regiment. The Army Reserve still uses parts of the castle to this day; the castle also houses Cumbria's Museum of Military Life.

Numerous ghosts are said to haunt the castle including King Stephen of England who lost Carlisle Castle to King David I of Scotland in 1135, and Mary, Queen of Scots who was imprisoned there for a few months in 1568. There is also a story of a spectral 'white lady' whose appearance has startled several sentries over the years. One tale dated to 1842 tells of a sentry who challenged the ghost and when she failed to stop, he lunged at her, only for the figure to fade away before his eyes. The poor sentry was discovered collapsed on the ground, his musket with fixed bayonet impaled in the wall.

It has been suggested that the spirit he and other sentries have encountered is the ghost of the woman whose skeleton dressed in a few shreds of silk tartan with valuable rings on her fingers is claimed to have been found bricked up in a wall of the Captain's Tower or the second storey of the keep in the 1830s. Curiously her feet were found resting on silk kerchiefs; there were no clues to her identity but it was strongly suspected that she had been walled up alive.

More frequently encountered are the ghostly echoes of noises, disembodied voices and footsteps of the soldiers who were at Carlisle Castle in the past. Soldiers love a prank or two and the stories of the 'White Lady' were built up and occasionally sentries would be 'spooked' by phantom footsteps or noises made by their pals hiding nearby. When soldiers laid their kit out on their army beds in prescribed military fashion for inspection, items of kit would occasionally go missing. A boot brush being used to polish a pair of army boots might be put down for a moment by the soldier only for it to disappear when he puts his hand down for it a moment later. A prank, perhaps, but this was known to happen when there really was no one near the soldier.

Each brush and in fact most items in a soldier's kit would be stamped or stencilled with his army number so there would be little point one of his mates nicking the item. It also meant if the item did disappear and turn up somewhere else, it would be recognisable from the unique number of the soldier stamped on it. This was often known to happen at Carlisle Castle, and not just to new recruits. Could it just be put down to soldiers' pranks or was there more to it? Could the spirit of a soldier or soldiers of the past be coming back and making mischief among the living soldiers?

Jacobites were held at the castle and were left without treatment for any injuries they may have sustained in fetid, damp cells for months on end in the knowledge that the way it would probably end for them would be on the end of an executioner's rope. Often left without food or water for long periods, they were reported to lick the walls of the condensation which gathered there and their only toilet facility was the floor.

Among them was 'Black Jock' Forbes of Inverernan, the Earl of Mar's baillie, who fought for the Jacobite cause as an officer in Mar's army. Jock was wounded and captured at the Battle of Sheriffmuir on 13 November 1715. Held at Carlisle Castle he was tried for treason and condemned to death but the night before his execution, on 8 November 1716, he chose to die by his own hand.

In 1746 many Jacobite prisoners were crammed into those cells after defeat at the Siege of Carlisle. During the winter of 1746 over thirty of them would be taken to the gallows on Harraby Hill where they suffered the death reserved for traitors as a dread warning to all. They were hanged by their neck until nearly dead, then cut down and their innards drawn from their bodies which were then hacked into quarters with an axe. Hundreds of spectators came to watch.

It is no wonder with such desperation and dread experienced within those walls staff at the castle have spoken of hearing groans, voices and even calls for help emanating from the cells where the Jacobites were held. Soldiers, whether they knew of the castle's dark past or not, would also speak of experiencing 'an air of dread and paranoia' for no apparent reason while at Carlisle Castle – a feeling far darker than any fright stirred up the pranks of living or dead soldiers.

Research by the author has revealed a surprising number of soldiers committed suicide at Carlisle Castle during the second half of the nineteenth and early twentieth centuries. The *Carlisle Patriot* records the tragic story of army pensioner, Michael Campton, a former member of the 95th Regiment, who was employed and given a residence at the castle to clean the arms and accoutrements of the Carlisle Artillery Volunteers. Michael had not been seen on the morning of Monday 25 June 1866 when he would usually be working. At 4 p.m. Sergeant-Major Rodney's children came to their father saying they had found him, adding, 'Michael is standing in his house with his face against the wall but won't speak.' Sergeant Jones went to investigate and found the old soldier 'suspended by a scarf about a yard long to one of the barrack pins'. Jones summoned assistance and the body was cut down. Dr Temperley was soon in attendance and pronounced life extinct. It was noted, however:

> The position in which he was found was rather peculiar. There was no chair or stool in such a position as to warrant the supposition that the deceased had stood upon it and then kicked it from under his feet. The conjecture, therefore, is that deceased had raised himself by his arms (which were stretched above his head) and thus prevented his feet from touching the ground, which they must have done had some means not been adopted.[1]

Quarter-Master Sergeant William Webster (50) had spent a lifetime in military service. He had served twenty-one years in the Royal Marine Artillery, and eleven years with 4th Battalion, the Border Regiment (Westmorland Militia). In November 1883 Webster shot himself in the quartermaster's stores at Carlisle Castle, with a Martini Henry rifle. Several of the garrison heard the shot and were soon in the room, 'They found him breathing heavily, but it was evident from the state of his skull, the bullet having entered the forehead, that life could only be of short duration.' Dr Lamb, the brigade surgeon, was at once brought to the scene of the painful occurrence, and Webster was removed to the hospital where he died within half an hour. A slip of paper was found in the office, in front of the deceased, bearing the message: 'Can't do my work. Memory gone and eyesight failing.'[2]

Sergeant Robert Marshall (50) of the Border Regiment had been acting as provost-sergeant for some time. He had attended the Artillery Volunteers' ball but the following day, 2 January 1902, he was in charge of the canteen; he bolted the door and was found later when others managed to gain entry through a window and he was found hanging by the neck by a bell rope (with one foot touching the floor) from a gas pipe in the short passage between the barroom and the billiard room in the sergeants' mess at the castle. He left a wife and eight children. The inquest returned a verdict of 'Suicide whilst temporarily insane'.[3]

Even as late as April 1922 Private Walter Bevins (18), the Border Regiment, committed suicide by hanging himself in the barracks at the castle. Sergeant Hewith stated at the inquest:

> During the last ten days deceased had been attending the military hospital for an abrasion on his knee. He had been depressed and during the last two or three days had not spoken to any of his comrades.

The coroner recorded a verdict of 'Suicide by hanging whilst temporarily insane'.[4]

Could the palpable but unexplained feeling of dread and paranoia that was known to descend on soldiers at the castle have been responsible for pushing these men over the edge? Or was it purely unfortunate circumstances that led them to end it all? If the sprits of soldiers linger and play tricks on the living, the soldiers who took their lives within its walls are, I think, prime candidates for those haunting Carlisle Castle.

Corby Castle, Corby, Cumbria

Corby Castle is a private residence and is not open to the public. The ghost story attached to it is a classic and deserves to be told. Today, Corby Castle looks more like a fine Georgian country house but it began as a red sandstone tower house built the Salkeld family in the thirteenth century. It was sold in 1611 to Lord William Howard (1563–1640), who built a two-storey, L-shaped house onto the peel tower; the present façade was added by Henry Howard (1757–1842) in the early nineteenth century. If you wish to view the property look out the five-part BBC dramatisation of Wilkie Collins's supremely spooky ghost story, *The Woman in White*, made in 1981 which used the castle as a location.

The story of the well-attested haunting at Corby Castle has appeared in many books over the years, one of the earliest accounts being in Mrs Catherine Crowe's *Night Side of Nature*, first published in 1848 in which she claims to have copied the account from a book of manuscript extracts dated 1824, loaned to her by a friend of the family. The published account has the names and locations shown as initials and blanks, but they have been worked out reliably and the reverend gentleman central to the story has been confirmed over the years, so I have filled in the blanks as appropriate:

> In order to introduce my readers to the haunted room, I will mention that it forms part of the old house, with windows looking into the court, which in early times was deemed a necessary security against an enemy. It adjoins a tower built by the Romans for defence; for Corby was properly more a border tower than a castle of any consideration. There is a winding staircase in this tower, and the walls are from eight to ten feet thick.
>
> When the times became more peaceable, our ancestors enlarged the arrow-slit windows and added to that part of the building which looks toward the river Eden; the view of which, with its beautiful banks, we now enjoy. But many additions and alterations have been made since that.
>
> To return to the room in question, I must observe that it is by no means remote or solitary, being surrounded on all sides by chambers that are constantly inhabited. It is accessible by a passage cut through a wall eight feet in thickness, and its dimensions are twenty-one by eighteen. One side of the wainscoting is covered with tapestry; the remainder is decorated with old family-pictures, and some ancient pieces of embroidery, probably the handiwork of nuns. Over a press, which has doors of Venetian glass, is an ancient oaken figure, with a battle-axe in his hand, which was one of those formerly placed on the walls of the city of Carlisle, to represent guards.
>
> There used to be, also, an old-fashioned bed and some dark furniture in this room; but, so many were the complaints of those who slept there, that I was induced to replace some of these articles of furniture by more modern ones, in the hope of removing a certain air of gloom, which I thought might have given rise to the unaccountable reports of apparitions and extraordinary noises which were constantly reaching us. But I regret to say I did not succeed in banishing the nocturnal visitor, which still continues to disturb our friends.

I shall pass over numerous instances, and select one as being especially remarkable, from the circumstance of the apparition having been seen by a clergyman well known and highly respected in this county, who, not six weeks ago, repeated the circumstances to a company of twenty persons, among whom were some who had previously been entire disbelievers in such appearances.

The best way of giving you these particulars, will be by subjoining an extract from my journal, entered at the time the event occurred.

Sept. 8, 1803. – Among other guests invited to Corby Castle, came the Rev. Henry Askew, Rector of Greystoke, with Mrs. Anne Askew, his wife, who was a Miss Sunderland, of Ulverstone. According to previous arrangements, they were to have remained with us for some days; but their visit was cut short in a very unexpected manner. On the morning after their arrival, we were all assembled at breakfast, when a chaise and four dashed up to the door in such haste that it knocked down part of the fence of my flower-garden. Our curiosity was, of course, awakened to know who could be arriving at so early an hour; when, happening to turn my eyes toward Reverend Askew, I observed that he appeared extremely agitated. 'It is our carriage!' said he; 'I am very sorry, but we must absolutely leave you this morning.'

We naturally felt and expressed considerable surprise, as well as regret at this unexpected departure; representing that we had invited Colonel and Mrs. S——, some friends whom Reverend Askew particularly desired to meet, to dine with us on that day. Our expostulations, however, were vain; the breakfast was no sooner over than they departed, leaving us in consternation to conjecture what could possibly have occasioned so sudden an alteration in their arrangements. I really felt quite uneasy lest anything should have given them offence; and we reviewed all the occurrences of the preceding evening in order to discover, if offence there was, whence it had arisen. But our pains were vain; and after talking a great deal about it for some days, other circumstances banished it from our minds.

It was not till we some time afterward visited the part of the country in which Reverend Askew resides, that we learned the real cause of his sudden departure from Corby. The relation of the fact, as it here follows, is in his own words: –

'Soon after we went to bed, we fell asleep: it might have been between one and two in the morning when I awoke. I observed that the fire was totally extinguished; but although that was the case, and we had no light, I saw a glimmer in the centre of the room, which suddenly increased to a bright flame. I looked out, apprehending that something had caught fire, when, to my amazement, I beheld a beautiful boy, clothed in white, with bright locks, resembling gold, standing by my bedside, in which position he remained some minutes, fixing his eyes upon me with a mild and benevolent expression. He then glided gently away toward the side of the chimney, where it is obvious there is no possible egress, and entirely disappeared. I found myself again in total darkness, and all remained quiet until the usual hour of rising. I declare this to be a true account of what I saw at Corby Castle, upon my word as a clergyman.'

I am acquainted with some of the family, and with several of the friends of Reverend Askew, who is still alive, though now an old man, and I can most positively assert that his own conviction, with regard to the nature of this appearance, has remained ever unshaken. The circumstance made a lasting impression upon his mind, and he never willingly speaks of it; but when he does, it is always with the greatest seriousness, and he never shrinks from avowing his belief, that what he saw admits of no other interpretation than the one he then put upon it.[5]

Greystoke Castle, Penrith, Cumbria

Greystoke Castle is primarily a private home where there is no public access. It is occasionally open for guided tours or hire as a wedding venue or for special events. The first stone structure on the site was built in 1129; it grew to become a large pele tower in the fourteenth century after William de Greystoke obtained a royal licence to crenellate it. It passed to the Howard family and has remained in their hands since the sixteenth century. In 1920 the *Evening News* published extracts from *A Social Diary of a Lady of Fashion* picked up in a second-hand bookshop in London. Along with some wonderful insights into her times, there was a ghost story from Greystoke Castle:

> Farrer [Sir Farrer Herschell, Solicitor-General, afterwards Lord Chancellor] is quite delighted because he has seen a ghost, or, to be more correct, because he has heard one. He was staying at Greystoke Castle with the Howards, and his bedroom was immediately over the front entrance.
>
> Farrer had been with Mr Howard to a political meeting in the evening and did not get to his room until about one o'clock in the morning. Just after he had put out his light, he heard a carriage drive up to the door; the gravel was very loose, and the wheels made a considerable noise. After a short time, he heard it drive away again, He thought that someone must have been taken ill in the house, and that the doctor had been sent for, but he thought it odd that his host should not have mentioned the circumstance. However, he went to sleep but awakened again at six o'clock to hear the carriage drive up again.
>
> So, he remarked to his wife, ''Somebody must be very ill, for that is the doctor again, I presume,' but she told him that she knew that the carriage had been ordered at that hour to take some of the guests to the station to catch an early train.
>
> Farrer mentioned at breakfast about having heard the carriage drive up in the middle of the night, and Lady Mabel Howard replied, 'That was our ghostly carriage. Our guests hear it not infrequently, but fortunately it does not appear to portend evil, so we don't mind how often it is heard.'[6]

Lancaster Castle, Lancaster, Lancashire

Lancaster Castle was founded in the eleventh century, and it has been both fortress and prison. It is entered through a particularly impressive 66-feet-high gatehouse built in the early fifteenth century. As a castle it repelled attack by the Scots in 1389 and saw action during the Civil War in 1643 when it was captured by Parliamentarian forces. As a prison many infamous individuals were held within its walls. Between 1782 and 1865, over 260 people were publicly executed by hanging at Lancaster Castle. With all those centuries of history it is no surprise that the castle is haunted.

A lot of the activity seems to be residual hauntings where day-to-day events and sounds are occasionally replayed, or ghostly smells assault the noses of visitors. A ghostly Scottish army has even been seen marching up the cobbles towards the gatehouse. Clearly the level of the road has been raised over the years and consequently the road they would have known was a lot lower down and only half the bodies of the spectral Scots were visible.

Inside the castle, in the prison it is Cell 3 that appears to be the most haunted cell in the castle. Visitors have reported being pushed or their clothes pulled by unseen hands when in there. A disembodied arm has been seen when upon investigation no one was in the cell. Blue lights have been spotted hovering in mid-air and what was thought to be a bundle of clothes in the corner by one visitor, eerily formed into a human shape and then melted into the darkness as they stood there aghast.

Probably the most famous of all those to be held and tried at Lancaster Castle are the women (and a couple of men) from the Pendle Hill area who were charged with the murders of ten people by witchcraft. One of the central figures in the case was a woman known as 'Mother Demdike', real name Elizabeth Southerns (80). She was accused of practising witchcraft for over fifty years but she died in the dungeon at Lancaster Castle while awaiting trial. The remaining accused were tried before Lancaster Assizes on 18–19 August 1612. Nine of these, namely Alizon Device, Elizabeth Device, James Device, Anne 'Chattox' Whittle, Anne Redferne, Alice Nutter, Katherine Hewitt, John Bulcock and Jane Bulcock, were found guilty and were hanged at Gallows Hill (now part of Williamson Park) on 20 August 1612. Of all these only the ghost of Mother Demdike is believed to haunt the castle; her spectre has been seen many times and is even claimed to have been captured on camera.

Leasowe Castle, near Wallasey, Cheshire

Leasowe Castle – also known as Mockbeggar Hall – is now a hotel located on the north coast of the Wirrel peninsula overlooking Leasowe

Beach. E. Cuthbert Woods's booklet *Leasowe Castle, Its Owners and History* (1920) points out the stretch of coast on which the castle stands; it was notorious in its day for wrecking up to the early nineteenth century:

> On the Cheshire coast not far from Liverpool they will rob those who have escaped the perils of the sea and come safe on shore and mutilate dead bodies for the sake of rings and personal ornaments.

Woods also notes a Gothic monument was erected to commemorate a fatal accident near the spot where it occurred in Breck Road, but owing to widening the road at this point, it does not now occupy its original site. A stone in the wall bears the following inscription:

> Near this spot Mrs. BOODE of Leasowe Castle was killed by a fall from her pony-carriage April 21st, 1826. May ye who pass by respect this memorial of an awful dispensation and the affectionate tribute of an only child to perpetuate her dear mother's memory beyond the existence of that breast which will never cease to cherish it. Ah, may the sad remembrance which attaches to this spot impress on everyone this salutary warning: 'In the midst of life we are in death.'

The ghostly clatter of Mrs Boode's pony carriage has occasionally been heard in the area ever since. Leasowe Castle itself was originally built in 1593 by Ferdinando, the 5th Earl of Derby, A story said to date to those turbulent times relates how a father and son were captured by the castle's owner and fearing they would be put to death, the father killed his son and then ended his own life. The ghosts of father and son are said to return and have greeted the gaze of those sleeping at the castle as they appear standing over the bed.

Lowther Castle, Lowther near Penrith, Cumbria

The current Lowther Castle was built between 1806 and 1814 for William Lowther, 1st Earl of Lonsdale. Today it stands an impressive ruin that looks, without its roof and empty rooms, every bit the haunted castle. Our story, however, relates to the previous building on the site, Lowther Hall, that was built in the seventeenth century by Viscount Lonsdale. Sir James Lowther (1736–1802), a noble lord known to history as 'Wicked Jimmy,' 'the Bad Earl' or, my personal favourite, 'Jemmy Graspall, Earl of Toadstool', inherited the Lowther estate in 1784. Most certainly an eccentric, he is known to have fought and survived at least two duels.

Sir James entered two arranged marriages in his lifetime but preferred to take mistresses. When he saw the beautiful daughter of one of his tenant farmers, he fell in love. She soon became his mistress, and he utterly adored her, but she fell ill and died. His lordship was inconsolable and rapidly became unhinged. He ordered his servants never to mention she was dead, her body was left to lie in bed as if sleeping and he was even known to dress her for dinner and have her sit at the dining table with him.

Eventually the stench of her decomposing body became too much, and Sir James had her placed in a coffin with a glass lid which he kept in a cupboard. Eventually she became so unsightly he allowed her to be buried.

Sir James sunk deeper into depression and it is thought he died of a broken heart. Various stories are told of his funeral where the coffin jerked around so much as it was borne by the pallbearers that they thought it was trying to spin over as the carried it. As the coffin was lowered into its grave, knocking and banging was heard from within and it was only held down with some difficulty as the earth was shovelled on top of it. An account by Jeremiah Sullivan published in 1857 claimed:

> Westmorland never produced a more famous boggle-infamous as a man, famous as a boggle – than Jemmy Lowther … a greater terror to the country after death, than he had been even during life. He was with difficulty buried; and whilst the clergyman was praying over him, he very nearly knocked the reverend gentleman from his desk. When placed in the grave, the power of creating alarm was not interred with his bones. There were disturbances in the hall, noises in the stables; neither men nor animals were suffered to rest. Jemmy's 'coach and six' is still remembered and spoken of … There is nothing said of his shape, or whether he appeared at all; but it is certain he made himself audible.

> The hall became almost uninhabitable, and out of the doors there was constant danger of meeting the miscreant ghost.[7]

For those unfamiliar with the term 'boggle' Sullivan offers a definition:

> As the word boggle includes all the varieties of the apparition kind that preceded it, so nothing is more uncertain than the manner in which the spirit manifests itself. Any shape, human, or animal, or composite, any unaccountable noise, may be a boggle.[8]

Sullivan goes on to explain how a Roman Catholic priest was called in to perform an exorcism in Latin at Lowther Castle, but the ghost held out against him until the spirit offered to go for a year and a day. The priest would not accept any compromise and read on until it appeared that he had successfully laid the spirit under a large stone. The rite does not appear to have been as successful as hoped and the ghost of 'Wicked Jimmy' is still said to appear on the anniversary of his death on 24 May if the moon is full. His ghost drives a spectral carriage at breakneck speed through Askham and Helton, whipping the ungroomed horses into a frenzy with their mouths frothing at their bits, until it heads up Loadpot Hill where the carriage fades away.

Muncaster Castle, Muncaster, Ravenglass, Cumbria

The Muncaster estate was granted to Alan de Penitone in 1208 and has remained in the hands of the Pennington family ever since. After the Battle of Hexham in 1464 Henry VI fled to the castle and Sir John Pennington gave safe shelter to the king. As a mark of his gratitude Henry gifted Sir John a fine Venetian drinking bowl made of green glass; it measures some six inches in diameter and is finely decorated with a gilded design. A verse traditionally attached to it promises:

> *It shall bless thy bed, it shall bless thy board,*
> *They shall prosper by this token,*
> *In Muncaster Castle, good luck shall be*
> *Till this charmed cup is broken.*

Another verse states:

As long as this bowl remains unriven,
Penningtons from Muncaster never shall be driven.

The bowl, known as the Luck of Muncaster, still exists; it is still in the castle and most importantly it is still intact. Henry VI died – he was probably murdered – in the Tower of London in May 1471. His ghost is said to appear in the Tower of London but is also haunts the chamber at Muncaster Castle that he occupied after Hexham.

The king is not the only spirit in the castle. One of the most frequently seen is the ghost of the 'White Lady', believed to be a Mary Bragg, a housekeeper in Ravenglass who was murdered in November 1805. The local story is Mary had found her true love in a footman at the castle but one of the housemaids also felt the same way and was determined her love rival should be removed from the picture.

On the night of 8 November 1805 two men came to the house where Mary worked to inform her that her lover was gravely ill and they would take her to his bedside. She left immediately but as they walked up a quiet road not far from the entrance to the castle grounds they murdered her near a large tree. Mary's body was found floating in the River Esk on 15 November. According to the story her head was so badly damaged and partially eaten away by eels, that the coroner could not tell exactly how she had died. According to account of the inquest published in the *Cumberland Pacquet* of 19 November 1805 Ravenglass surgeons John Bragg and John Taylor had examined Mary's body:

> They found no marks of violence that could explain her death and confirmed that the blue linen handkerchief around her neck was, even when soaked, 'so loose and fastened in such a manner that it could not occasion her Death or have been the means of strangling her'. There were no marks on the neck to suggest that the handkerchief had at any time been pulled tighter to strangle her, and they would also have expected her face to be a different colour if she had been strangled rather than drowned. There were, however, some marks on her arms with 'the appearance of being made or caused by the presence of fingers while the deceased was

> living' which the doctors could not explain, but seemed most likely to have been caused by Mary herself, for there were no corresponding marks of thumbs on the opposite side of the arms, as would have been expected if someone gripped her.

Mary's father, Henry Bragg, stated at the inquest that he strongly believed Sarah Jackson and John Pickthall, both of Muncaster House 'could give material information and are necessary witnesses'. It does not appear either were called. The *Paquet* initially reported the inquest verdict had been Mary Bragg was 'found drowned and suffocated in the waters of the River Esk … but how or by what means she became drowned and suffocated as aforesaid is wholly unknown to the jurors'.

The *Cumberland Pacquet* of 26 November 1805, however, published the following:

> The paragraph in our last, concerning the body of a young woman, found at Muncaster-Steps, &c. was erroneous in several particulars. – We have indisputable authority for saying, that after the most minute examination by Mr Benson the coroner, two surgeons, and a respectable jury, there did not appear a single circumstance to warrant an opinion of any violence or cruelty having been committed upon the body; but there were strong reasons for suspecting that the death of the unfortunate girl had been her own rash act. The jury returned a verdict – Found drowned.

When the tree where she was murdered was eventually cut down, it was said to have been seen to bleed a red fluid that looked very much like fresh blood. The ghost of Mary Bragg, the unavenged murder victim, still wanders the grounds of Muncaster. The ghost believed to be Mary has been seen late at night on the road near the castle on several occasions over recent years. More than one driver has stopped to check if the apparently solid figure of the woman was okay, only for her to disappear.

Thomas Skelton, the Fool of Muncaster, the jester reputed to be the original 'Tom Fool', has some wonderfully tall tales associated with him. Yes, take it with a pinch of salt, but it's a cracker that has been told by firelight in the area for generations. The tale set around 1600 (give or take fifty years), recounted in 'The Remains of John Briggs, a compilation of tales and essays' published in the *Westmorland Gazette and Lonsdale Magazine* in 1825, 'Wild Will' of Whitbeck had his mind set on marrying Helewise Pennington, the unmarried daughter of Sir Alan Pennington, the owner of Muncaster Castle. Helewise, however, had rebuffed the advances of Will in favour of handsome young Dick, a carpenter at the castle. Will knew Sir Ferdinand Hoddleston, of Millum Castle, who also sought the hand of Helewise, and knew he would be incensed to learn that she was favouring such a lowly individual. Will told Hoddleston who set off post haste to warn Sir Alan Pennington of his daughter's foolish choice of suitor. While on his way Hoddleston happened upon Tom Skelton, the castle fool. Apparently, he also had an axe to grind with Dick the carpenter, and according to Brigg's account, Tom said to Hoddleston:

> 'I put those three shillings which you gave me into a hole, and I found them weezend everytime I went to look at them; and now they are only three silver pennies. I have just found it out that Dick has weezend them.'
>
> 'Kill him Tom, with his own axe, when he is asleep sometime – and I'll see that thou takest no harm for it.' Replied Sir Ferdinand.
>
> 'He deserves it, and I'll do it,' said Tom …
>
> And the next day while the unsuspecting carpenter was taking an after dinner nap, and dreaming probably of the incomparable beauties of his adorable Helewise, Tom entered the shed, and with one blow of the axe severed the carpenters head from his body. 'There,' said Tom to the servants, 'I have hid Dick's head under a heap of shavings; and he will not find that so easily, when he awakes, as he did my shillings.'

According to the tale Helewise became a nun, and in some versions of the story the poor woman went mad. Tom Skelton never did pay for his crime, and his ghost is said to haunt Muncaster for evermore, with the severed head of poor Dick the carpenter in his hand.

Is it all just a myth? Patrick Gordon Duff Pennington who had inherited the castle and owned it until his death in 2021 thought it was until he heard footsteps following him in the hall of the castle on many occasions. He sought to explain it, wondering if they were an echo. Mr Duff Pennington attempted to emulate the steps and could never reproduce them. The mournful crying of a woman had also been heard through the doors of rooms that were on investigation found to be empty.

Many of the sightings and experiences at Muncaster Castle over recent years have centred around the Tapestry Room. The manifestations include a black, featureless figure and the sound of a child crying and sobbing has been heard near the window. Research has revealed the room had previously been a nursery. Peter Frost Pennington, the current owner of Muncaster Castle, told *The Whitehaven News* in 2011, 'The Tapestry Room used to be a guest bedroom for friends and family, but so many people ended up complaining of having ghostly experiences in the room that we had to stop using it.'[9] Several paranormal investigation teams have investigated the site over the years and their conclusion is Muncaster Castle is most certainly haunted.

Naworth Castle, Naworth, Cumbria

Naworth Castle probably originates from a thirteenth-century peel house that grew to become the castle worthy of the notorious Dacre family, Lord Wardens of the Marches. It passed by marriage to the Howard family in the sixteenth century, among them Lord William Howard known for his actions to bring the Border Reivers to heel, the 'Belted Will' mentioned by Walter Scott in his *Lay of the Last Minstrel* (1805):

Costly his garb – his Flemish ruff
Fell o'er his doublet, shaped of buff,
With sattin slashed, and lined;
Tawny his boot, and gold his spur,
His cloak was all of Poland fur,
His hose with silver twined;
His Bilboa blade, by Marchmen felt,
Hung in a broad and studded belt;

Hence, in rude phrase, the Borderers still
Called noble Howard, Belted Will.

A story handed down the years about 'Belted Will' is far from romantic. His men had captured several moss-troopers (brigands) and Will's faithful lieutenant reported the news to him while he was reading. Irritated at being disturbed, without even looking up from the volume in which he was engrossed, Will barked out a dismissive 'Hang them in the Devil's name.' And this his lieutenant saw to it was done and the prisoners were strung up from a tree outside the castle.

An article in the *Newcastle Courant* in February 1885 describes:

> The private apartments communicate by secret passages with the dungeons. Thus whilst reading in his library, or engaged in his confessional, his eyes might be directed towards his prisoners and his guards, so that it might be truly said of Naworth Castle that 'suspicion was its architect and fear its founder'.[10]

The corridors of Naworth Castle are haunted by a classic 'woman in white' ghost. The tale attached to why her spirit still walks dates to the time when the Dacres held the castle and tells of how she was a local girl who was seduced by and fell in love with the lord. When she fell pregnant with his child, he shunned her and she drowned herself in the lake.

Her mother cursed the lord, with the spell:

O curst be the cruel hand
That wrought this hour to me!
May evil grim aye follow him
Until the day he dee.

It was a curse said with such venom that can only come from a mother towards the one upon whom she blamed the death of her daughter. The tale tells of how Dacre died soon afterwards when he was garrotted by a thorn bush into which he had been thrown from horse. The Lord's heir would also die from the curse when he became mired in the soft mud around the lake where the girl had drowned herself. The more he struggled the deeper he sank until he was completely engulfed and was suffocated.

The hanged moss-troopers are occasionally seen wandering in the grounds and the 'woman in white' ghost of the cruelly deceived pregnant girl still drifts along the corridors, perhaps as a warning to subsequent lords and owners of Naworth Castle.

Sizergh Castle, Kendal, Cumbria

Sizergh Castle stands in Helsington in historic Westmorland, now part of Cumbria. The original fortification on the site can be traced to 1170 when Gervase d'Eyncourt was granted Sizergh by William de Lancaster, Lord of Kendal. An old tale tells oh how d'Eyncourt was a fierce warrior baron who no one dared to cross and, surprise, surprise, he was also an insanely jealous man. When summoned to fight the marauding Scots, he locked his wife Basilia away in a room of the tower and left strict instruction to his servants that none was to unlock that door on pain of death. None would dare disobey the order. The problem was it also meant that there was no way to get food to her and the unfortunate woman starved to death. Her ghostly, anguished cries and sobbing are said to still echo through the castle.

Sizergh became the principal residence of the Strickland family in 1239 and remained so into the twentieth century. The castle we see today originated from a fourteenth-century tower house or peel tower built on the site of an earlier structure. It has been expanded over the centuries to include a great hall from about 1450; two wings extending to the west were built in the sixteenth century that also created a courtyard.

Dynasties, marriages and allegiances were keys to power in the sixteenth century and the Stricklands were cousins of Katherine Parr (1512–48), twice married to noble gentlemen whom she outlived; her third husband was King Henry VIII. She was Henry's sixth and final wife and queen consort; she outlived him too and went on to marry Thomas Seymour of Sudeley.

Katherine Parr stayed with her cousins at Sizergh in the 1530s and is said to haunt the Queen's Room in the castle. Her appearances are quiet and subtle, so it does leave one wondering who or what is the most aggressive and frightening spirit in the castle? Could it simply be tall tales that got blown out of all proportion? At a time when there was discussion in the press about haunted houses in 1930, Lord Strickland wrote to *The Times*:

> When I was spending a first summer at Sizergh Castle, nearly half-a-century ago, the countryside believed it was 'haunted', and to keep servants a 'commissionaire' in uniform with a loaded revolver had to patrol at night. Gardeners and tenants were warned that the 'ghost' would be shot at [on] sight. I never saw there nor heard anything that, on reflection, savoured of the supernatural, but many others have said they did. An annual visitor, on her arrival, used to sit on the stairs till she was assured that her bedroom was not to be upstairs, because 'the ghost visits her in the attached bathroom'.

His lordship went on to state he had heard strange noises in the castle, but he was convinced they were just creaking timbers of the old house, gurgling pipework, death-watch beetles knocking and rats and mice behind the panelling.

That said, the belief in Sizergh Castle being haunted does go back a long way and was not just in the imaginations of impressionable servant girls as the *Lancashire Evening Post* rather haughtily commented in 1903, in a feature on Sizergh Castle; having described the state bedroom, the article went on to mention:

> The room above this is relegated to the use mainly of the Sizergh ghost, a young lady who, in the fancy of ignorant housemaids, walks about here at night. She is reputed to have been murdered in this room and betrays the usual singularly morbid taste of ghosts for places which must surely conjure up painful memories; nobody deserving of credence has ever seen her, nor can anyone be met who alleges to have done so. Through the haunted chamber the top of the tower, which is about 60ft. high, is reached. Thence there is fine view over the countryside, and especially the park itself.[11]

Clearly, the author of that article was not aware that forty years earlier an intrepid group of eighty gentlemen and ladies from the Kendal Literary and Scientific Institution became very much the ghost hunters of their day when they made an excursion to Sizergh Castle on Friday 27 July 1860. When it is considered that at that time no women wore trousers, corsets were worn as standard and crinoline cages were essential wear under their generous skirts, even under walking dresses specifically designed for the strolling through the countryside, it is not suspiring the women were particularly praised in the *Kendal Mercury* for their determination:

> The owner of the Castle, W. C. Strickland, Esq., had kindly given his sanction to the excursion, and every portion of the venerable and interesting structure was opened to the company. Every antient Castle has its ghost, and Sizergh is no exception. The room said to be its haunt is one of small dimensions, accessible only by means of ladders from the leads [the roof of the castle]. Great anxiety was manifested to inspect the spot chosen by the unearthly visitor, and an amount of enterprise and venturesomeness most exemplary was exhibited by many of the ladies, in gratifying their curiosity.[12]

Triermain Castle, Gilsland, Cumbria

I conclude this chapter on the haunted castles of the North West with the one that has the least of it left above ground. Looking more like an upright stone-built monument, all that remains visible of Triermain Castle is a solitary corner of its gatehouse. The ruins of an internal building also remain as do remnants of walls and earthworks under the ground but there is little to show of the enclosure castle, quadrangular in plan, with towers on the east and west sides, surrounded by a curtain wall and a moat that once stood there.

The castle was built by Hubert de Vaux who was granted the Barony of Gilsland by King Henry II for his services in France and in the campaign to recover Cumberland from the Scots in 1157. One of his descendants, Roland de Vaux was granted a licence to crenellate the property in 1340. The castle was never besieged nor subject to any serious attack but by the late sixteenth century it was in ruins. A survey conducted during the reign of Elizabeth I described Triermaine Castle as:

> a house of great strength and good receipt. It stood and was built opposite the wastes of Scotland and Tynedell … and was a very convenient place both for annoying of the enemie [the Scots] and defending the country thereabouts, but now the said castle is utterly decayed.

The castle tower was demolished in the late eighteenth century and large quantities of its stone was taken away and were used in the construction of farms and farm buildings in the area. Some would believe the castle had been doomed because a considerable amount of stone from the nearby Hadrian's Wall had been used in the construction and those stones carried with them an ancient curse that none would prosper in a house built of wall stone, and like the wall it too would turn to rubble. Others would believe the place had been damned because Roland's older brother, Hubert, a hard man so keen to acquire wealth and power, had turned to using dark arts to bring about the apparently 'accidental' and sudden deaths of his rivals.

Another tale tells of how a young boy had inherited the castle in the fourteenth century and he and the castle were placed in the safe keeping of his uncle until the boy came of age. If the boy didn't reach maturity his uncle would inherit it all. The uncle neglected the boy and starved him until he became very weak. One day when an icy cold wind and blizzard had set in, the wicked uncle left the boy in the middle of a moor where he froze to death. From that time forward when any of his family fell ill, the ghost of frozen boy would appear by their bed shivering and his teeth chattering. If they were going to die from the illness, the boy would lay his small, icy hand on the diseased part and say:

> *Cauld, cauld, aye, cauld.*
> *An ye'se be cauld for evermair.*

The castle and the Vaux family have been immortalised in Sir Walter Scott's poem *The Bridal of Triermain*, Samuel Taylor Coleridge's ballad *Christabel* and Robert Carlyle's poem *De Vaux, or the Heir of Gilsland.*

Chapter 2

The North East

Our Dob waved wand
He held in his hand,
And a legion of spirits appeared;
Good witches and bad,
Sane goblins and mad,
With fairy and sprite,
In red and in white.
And horrible ghoules
Attended by owls,
And wizards in cloaks,
The dread of young folks.

B. Clarke, *The Ballad of Briggy Dobby*

Alnwick Castle, Alnwick, Northumberland

The original Alnwick Castle was erected to command a road crossing of the River Aln by Norman nobleman Ivo de Vesci around 1096. It was then purchased by the Percy family, the earls and later the dukes of Northumberland, during the reign of Henry III (1207–72). The Percy family greatly enlarged the modest castle, making it both an impressive stronghold and a great symbol of the power of the Percy family. It has remained their property ever since.

Alnwick Castle has stood through the Wars of the Roses and the English Civil War; it was used by Oliver Cromwell to hold prisoners captured at the Battle of Dunbar in 1650. Within those historic walls when you wander through its stately rooms, you get an amazing sense of history, perhaps so much history no one spirit has established itself above all others and cannot even claim a well-known spectre of a 'woman in white' in its haunted heritage. That said, Alnwick castle undoubtedly has spirits and presences felt by those able to feel them and its does have a well-documented story of a vampire.

Fortunately, instances of vampires and vampirism are rare in Britain, but they *have* occurred. This case, often retold with embellishments or in an edited form, is the account as it was originally recorded by the chronicler William of Newburgh (1136–98) who obtained the story from those who had witnessed it personally. Written in Newburgh's *Historia Rerum Anglicarum*, it tells of how a dead master of Alnwick Castle, 'a stranger to God's race and whose crimes were many', rose from his tomb during the hours of darkness and stalked the streets of Alnwick as a vampire:

> A Christian burial, indeed, he received, though unworthy of it; but it did not much benefit him: for issuing, by the handiwork of Satan, from his grave at night-time, and pursued by a pack of dogs with horrible barkings, he wandered through the courts and around the houses while all men made fast their doors, and did not dare to go abroad on any errand whatever from the beginning of the night until the sunrise, for fear of meeting and being beaten black and blue by this vagrant monster. But those precautions were of no avail; for the atmosphere, poisoned by the vagaries of this foul carcass, filled every house with disease and death by its pestiferous breath.
>
> Already did the town, which but a short time ago was populous, appear almost deserted; while those of its inhabitants who had escaped destruction migrated to other parts of the country, lest they too should die. The man from whose mouth I heard these things, sorrowing over this desolation of his parish, applied himself to summon a meeting of wise and religious men on that sacred day which is called Palm Sunday, in order that they might impart healthful counsel in so great a dilemma, and refresh the spirits of the miserable remnant of the people with consolation, however imperfect. Having delivered a

discourse to the inhabitants, after the solemn ceremonies of the holy day had been properly performed, he invited his clerical guests, together with the other persons of honour who were present, to his table.

While they were thus banqueting, two young men (brothers), who had lost their father by this plague, mutually encouraging one another, said, 'This monster has already destroyed our father, and will speedily destroy us also, unless we take steps to prevent it. Let us, therefore, do some bold action which will at once ensure our own safety and revenge our father's death. There is no one to hinder us; for in the priest's house a feast is in progress, and the whole town is as silent as if deserted. Let us dig up this baneful pest, and burn it with fire.'

Thereupon snatching up a spade of but indifferent sharpness of edge, and hastening to the cemetery, they began to dig; and whilst they were thinking that they would have to dig to a greater depth, they suddenly, before much of the earth had been removed, laid bare the corpse, swollen to an enormous corpulence, with its countenance beyond measure turgid and suffused with blood; while the napkin in which it had been wrapped appeared nearly torn to pieces. The young men, however, spurred on by wrath, feared not, and inflicted a wound upon the senseless carcass, out of which incontinently flowed such a stream of blood, that it might have been taken for a leech filled with the blood of many persons.

Then, dragging it beyond the village, they speedily constructed a funeral pile; and upon one of them saying that the pestilential body would not burn unless its heart were torn out, the other laid open its side by repeated blows of the blunted spade, and, thrusting in his hand, dragged out the accursed heart. This being torn piecemeal, and the body now consigned to the flames, it was announced to the guests what was going on, who, running thither, enabled themselves to testify henceforth to the circumstances. When that infernal hell-hound had thus been destroyed, the pestilence which was rife among the people ceased, as if the air, which had been corrupted by the contagious motions of the dreadful corpse, were already purified by the fire which had consumed it.

Bamburgh Castle, Bamburgh, Northumberland

Situated betwixt a rolling landscape of fields and countryside, and a wide sandy shoreline by the sea, Bamburgh Castle is undoubtedly one of the most picturesque castles in the country. With such a command over land and sea, a fortification has stood on the Bamburgh headland since the time of the Celts in the fifth century AD, but the old wooden fort was destroyed by the Vikings in 993.

The Normans built a new castle on the site with a great stone keep erected in 1164. Impregnable to early sieges, warfare changed and as cannon became prevalent Bamburgh became the first English castle to fall to artillery fire after a nine-month-long siege by Richard Neville, 16th Earl of Warwick in 1464. The castle remained in ruins until restoration was begun in the eighteenth century, but it would only be in the nineteenth century, after the castle came into the ownership of wealthy northern industrialist William Armstrong who had the finances to sink into the castle, that it would be fully restored.

The castle is decorated in a medieval baronial style as imagined by a Victorian gentleman but it still has plenty of atmosphere and invisible presences are often felt there. The ghost of a knight in armour is said to clank around the castle. The ghost of a daughter of the house, heartbroken having not been allowed to marry the man she loved, has been seen wearing a green cloak, her ghost throwing itself from the battlements but fading away before it hits the ground below.

In April 1936 *Sunday Sun* reporter James R. Spencer was shown around Bamburgh Castle by Lord Armstrong who related the following story of one of the least-known castle ghosts, that of Dr John Sharp, Archdeacon of Northumberland (1693–1758), who used to live in the castle:

> A chauffeur going along a corridor of the castle said he saw someone coming along. He said at the time it was Lady Armstrong. The man stepped aside into an alcove in the passage to allow the person to pass. He kept his eyes down and caught a glimpse of buckled shoes.
>
> He had been ordered to drive Lady Armstrong that afternoon, so he went downstairs and asked for her ladyship. And judge of the man's surprise when it was

> pointed out to him that she was at that moment walking on the beach quite a long way away. He could see Lady Armstrong for himself on the beach, through one of the castle windows. … The sequel to this experience, Lord Armstrong told me, was that the man was taken into the King's Hall, where a number of oil paintings are hanging, and the man was asked to look at them. Immediately he picked out the portrait of Archdeacon Sharp, who of course, had been dead many scores of years, as the picture of the person who passed him in the passage. And in the picture, you can see the buckled shoes quite clearly.[1]

Bamburgh Castle often seems to have a great deal of birds circling above it, much like the castle described by *Dracula* author Bram Stoker in his last novel, *The Lair of the White Worm.* Bram's distant Stoker ancestors came from Northumberland, and it is tempting to imagine he did visit the place and was inspired by the sight. The area is certainly known for the old legend of 'The Laidly Worm of Spindleston Heugh'. Stoker even mentioned the tale in his book. Worm is a medieval word for serpent-like dragons that often grew to huge sizes and would lay waste to the land they inhabited. In this story the worm is the beautiful Princess Margaret who was turned into the creature by an evil witch (some accounts say she was the princess's wicked stepmother), using the enchantment:

> *I weird ye to be a Laidly Worm,*
> *And borrowed shall ye never be,*
> *Until Childe Wynd, the King's own son*
> *Come to the Heugh and thrice kiss thee;*
> *Until the world comes to an end,*
> *Borrowed shall ye never be.*

The errant knight Childe Wynd had been away on campaign overseas and returned to discover the land in a sorry state, but suspecting witchcraft had been afoot rather than slaying the worm with his sword, he kissed it and the princess was restored to her human form again. The knight turns the witch into a toad, he marries the princess and he becomes king; all is well across the land, and it flourishes again.

Barnard Castle, Barnard Castle, County Durham

Barnard Castle was built in stone by the Balliol family during the first half of the twelfth century on land gifted to them by King William Rufus. Sited of a commanding eminence above the River Tees, the castle was built to control the river crossing between the territory of the Bishop of Durham and the Honour of Richmond.

Later owners included the earls of Warwick and from 1471 the castle passed to Richard, Duke of Gloucester who later became King Richard III. Richard's heraldic emblem of the white boar can still be seen carved above a window in the great chamber overlooking the river.

During the 'Rising of the North' in December 1569 the castle was besieged and bombarded by a force of 5,000 men in support of Mary, Queen of Scots. Sir George Bowes and his garrison of around 700 men held the castle in the name of Elizabeth I but was forced to surrender it after eleven days. The castle was never rebuilt; it went into decline and was pretty much abandoned by the eighteenth century.

One local story tells of 'Lady Ann Day', not a name that immediately springs out of the historical records of the castle, but it is claimed she was murdered and thrown from the battlements. Her heavily bloodstained ghost is said to occasionally be seen falling down the side of the castle. In another tale the woman wears a red cloak and she is not actually murdered but accidently drowned when her husband stumbled as he carried across the river on his shoulders.

The paranormal activity around the castle takes the form of cold spots, presences and misty, shapeless entities rather than having a particular being attributed to a particular incident or individual as their cause. Thus many have some connection to the fact that that area was once infamous for hauntings and witchcraft. In a feature titled 'At Barnard Castle' the *Teesdale Mercury* explained in 1878:

> The student of folk-lore will find a rich harvest lying to his hand. Tales of ghosts, boggles, and fairies, of witches, warlocks, spunkies and kelpies, of elf-candles, dead-lights, wraiths, warnings, cantraips, and apparitions, of glamour, evil eyes, and ill-bespokes, and all the rest of the queer things and queer folks who peopled out-of-the-way places

> and played such queer tricks in the days before the invention of gas and the steam engine.[2]

All but forgotten today the local bogeyman in 'Barny' in the eighteenth and nineteenth centuries was a demonic lantern man known as Briggy Dobbie who would appear when you least expected it or could be summoned by the foolhardy when his name was said thrice in quick succession (*à la* Beetlejuice), his name or image used in a prank or said in mockery. There were many tales of this devilish creature and even a local ballad. The *Teesdale Mercury* explained in an article published in 1879:

> Fifty years ago it would have been unnecessary at Barnard Castle to attempt to describe the 'Briggy Dobbie'. Many people would have averred that they had seen it; many more that they believed in it. Now, however, 'the schoolmaster is abroad', old beliefs are dying out; apparitions, generally, are at a discount; and to the majority of the rising generation the Briggy Dobbie – if they have heard of it at all – is but a name. ... The Briggy Dobbie, then we may explain was the barguest or town's ghost. It was of portentous aspect, dark visaged, rattling a chain as it glided along, and attended by a lurid light. ... In its more frolicsome moods the Briggy Dobbie assumed the shape of a huge black dog, and was in the habit of seizing upon belated topers when they returned home from their carousals, and rolling them in the gutter, At least the revellers often assigned that reason to their wives for their dirty and confused appearance; but whether the wives implicitly believed all the particulars or not, is an open question. The Briggy-Dobbie, in each of its forms was dreaded, and it was considered unlucky to meet it.[3]

Bellister Castle, near Haltwhistle, Northumberland

Bellister Castle began as a fourteenth-century tower house that was enlarged with additions over the following centuries when it was in the hands of the Blenkinsop family. The property is not open to the public, but it is the outside where the hauntings take place. One tale tells of seven 'bold moss troopers' being hanged from a sycamore on the castle mound who still wander the area. The other is one of the classic ghostly tales of the Borders – 'The Grey Man of Bellister'. The following is an edited version of the story, which has been dated to 1470, published in the *Newcastle Chronicle* 1895:

> The tradition runs that many centuries ago, when the castle stood in its then impregnable strength, and its lord was the proud owner of all the fertile fields – round about, one stormy afternoon, when darkness was fast setting in, the porter at the gate was addressed by a wandering minstrel, an aged grey-haired man, who sought shelter for the night. The baron having been appealed to, readily gave the poor wayfarer leave to stay, and moreover directed him to be brought into the hall, where supper was being set out.
>
> After this meal had been despatched and the tables cleared the minstrel was called upon to regale them with quaint old tales and ballads to the accompaniment of his harp and much it was enjoyed too. The Baron of Bellister, however, was a man of suspicious temperament, and so, while the minstrel was running his fingers deftly across the strings of the harp, and singing, in a voice somewhat broken by age, the Baron sat knitting his brows, for a dark thought had entered his mind. Might not this stranger, who had arrived at such an untimely hour, and who had an eye in his head as keen as a hawk's, with which he seemed to be glancing round furtively, to take the measure of all he saw in and about the place, whenever he thought himself unobserved – might he not be a secret spy, sent to ferret out dangerous secrets, by a neighbouring baron, with whom he had long been at feud?
>
> The longer he sat, and the more the Baron thought of it, the stronger and deeper his suspicions grew. Every movement the poor minstrel made only served to confirm them. When all had retired for the night, the baron continued to pace his room. At length, having worked himself up into a passion, he summoned his attendants, and directed them to bring the old minstrel into his presence so he could question

him. They went accordingly to the bedchamber where the minstrel should have been sleeping but found that it was empty and he had fled the castle. By this act the baron's suspicions, in his mind at least, were confirmed.

The Baron ordered out his bloodhounds and the pursuit of the fugitive commenced. The dogs soon got upon the man's track and had not far to run before they came upon him at a clump of willow trees near the banks of the Tyne and they pulled him down. The foremost of the pursuing party could not reach the old minstrel before the hounds had torn him to pieces. Whether the baron's suspicions had been well founded, or whether they had been engendered solely by his own morbid imagination, no mortal could ever tell. But remorse for the barbarous outrage gripped the baron, who never had a single day's peace of mind after that.

Wherever he went, he was never alone. The grey-haired old minstrel, horrible in his disfigurement, became his companion. His own shadow was much more fitful in its attendance on him, for it went and came with the light, whether of the sun, the moon, the fire, or the lamp. The ghost was most dreadful when it could not be seen, when its cold, unnerving presence only was felt, when it stalked behind the baron's back. At length the baron 'slept with his fathers', and by-and-by his race became extinct.

The castle and grounds passed into other hands, innocent of the minstrel's blood. Yet, nevertheless, the goblin still haunted the place, as if where a foul, unprovoked, and unavenged murder had been committed, it had a perfectly good right and title to walk, even till the crack of doom. Sometimes it made its appearance harmlessly to one or other of the inmates of the castle when going to or coming from the neighbouring ferry or ford; at other times it was seen stalking round the old building, with an aspect more terrific and threatening than usual; and then it always betokened impending misfortune or death.[4]

Mr William Pattison, of Sunderland added to the tale in Richardson's *Local Historian's Table Book of Remarkable Occurrences* (1841), recounting the story of when a young man came to seek employment at Bellister Castle:

> Having crossed the Tyne at Haltwhistle, he found the darkness increasing fast, and although the distance he had to travel was not great, yet, in those days, bad companions were more common than welcome on the unfrequented roads after nightfall. Leaving the ferry, he passed a thicket of willow bushes, and then his route lay along a broken road, which he had been directed to follow as that which would conduct him to the castle. He had not proceeded far when he descried a traveller at some little distance in advance. … He therefore quickened his pace, and, when sufficiently near, shouted to the unknown individual to stop. But the stranger paid no regard – he neither stopped nor looked behind. The lad had now approached within a few yards, yet with the utmost exertion he could not overtake him. He passed forward with superhuman rapidity, gliding rather than walking over the surface.
>
> An unpleasant sensation of fear crept over the youth, which was not a little increased, by a closer inspection, as far as the dubious light enabled, of the object of his misgivings. His head was uncovered, and his long hair hung behind, white as the frosts of winter. He was rapt in a long grey cloak, reaching to his heels, and he appeared to carry a small bundle under his arm, concealed by his exterior vestments. So occupied had the youth been in the stranger, that he did not perceive that he had now reached the broken gateway of the old Castle of Bellister. At that very moment when its dark mass became evident through the investing gloom, the mysterious figure unexpectedly stood still, and turning abruptly round upon the youth, revealed the awful nature of the fellowship, which he, in the simplicity of his heart, was so eager to obtain.
>
> Death had set his pallid seal on that grisly countenance, and a bloody gash that ran across it heightened the expression of ghastliness imprinted there. The thick beard was dripping with blood, and the fore part of its garments was dyed with

the ensanguined stream. It fixed its large lustreless eyes upon the youth, and, pointing with a hideous scowl towards the dilapidated ruin, melted silently away. It was a scene of the deepest horror.

His new home was nigh and without thinking more he went there. The old mistress was the only one of the family within, and to her he recounted the horrifying apparition he had witnessed. The old lady was much concerned. She knew of the ghost and that he was never seen without some accompanying calamity, and when, as on the present occasion, there was manifested tokens of a vindictive disposition on the spirit's part, the danger was near and alarming. It came to pass as the old lady feared and predicted. That very evening the unfortunate lad was seized with an illness, and before next morning was a corpse.[5]

Blenkinsopp Castle, Greenhead, Northumberland

The 'castle' located not far from Haltwhistle and close to the Cumbrian border, like many of the 'castles' in this once dangerous borderland, is in fact a thirteenth-century fortified manor house, founded by Randolph de Blenkinsopp. In the late nineteenth century, the castle was incorporated in a Victorian Gothic-style mansion by Lord Joicey of Etal but much of this was destroyed by a terrible fire in 1954.

The tradition at Blenkinsopp Castle was that when its occupier was about to die, the event would always be heralded by the appearance of a huge black hound on not just one but two occasions. The first time, before the death the dog would be seen standing in the grounds looking into the house or even standing looking as solid as any earthy dog in a corridor inside, but the second time it came in more spectral form and would glide through the chamber of death as the spirit of the dying master made its departure.

The castle's best-known haunting is that of the 'White Woman' ghost which finds its origins in the mid-fifteenth century when Brian de Blenkinsopp lived there. This account of the tale is based on the version recorded by Paul Brown published in the *Newcastle Chronicle* in December 1939:

Brian was in many respects, a fortunate young man. He was good looking, wealthy and brave. If he was masterful, rude when he felt like it, and keen on the bawbees [Scottish sixpence], there was not getting away from the fact that he was a very eligible young gentleman. It is said that the marriageable ladies of the neighbourhood gave him the glad eye.

But Brian set a high value upon himself as a husband and saw no reason for giving himself away. He made it known that any girl set on marrying him must throw into the bargain a chest full of treasure so weighty that it would require ten men to heave it into the castle.

The Squire of Blenkinsopp remained a bachelor until he went to fight under Henry V at Agincourt. Brian eventually returned to Blenkinsopp with a wife! If that shock was not severe enough there was another following close upon its heels. There were those in the village that twelve men had been seen carrying a huge treasure-chest into the castle. They certainly wondered who on earth could the woman be? But they never got to know.

The Lady of Blenkinsopp was seldom seen and showed no inclination to mix in local society. All that was known about her was that she dressed in white, which did not suit her complexion, and that she had a particularly bright pair of dangerous looking eyes. Then it leaked out that although she had brought the box of treasure with her, Brian was not a shareholder. Whenever he wanted to borrow the key, his wife told him, in the presence of her twelve henchmen, that if his idea of matrimonial bliss was entertaining his free-booting cronies on her money, he had better think again.

One day Brian came home to discover that while he had been absent his wife had set those servants of hers to work, digging a hole somewhere underneath the Castle, and in that hole her dowry, box and all its contents, had been buried. She refused to tell him where the treasure was, and her servants were sworn to silence. Brian went down the winding stairs of the castle four at a time, bounced out of the house, and

> slammed the front door behind him and was never seen nor heard of again. His lady had not expected this. After all a husband was a husband and goodness knew what he might be up to. So, one day she and her faithful twelve, rode away from Blenkinsopp in search of the missing man.
>
> Where they went and whether they ever found him nobody ever learned but this was known, they did not take the treasure with them. What became of it? Many people have looked for it in Blenkinsopp Castle. Several times seekers have believed themselves to be on the right track. It is even said that, in ghostly form, of the 'White Lady' comes seeking it too on moonlit nights. Some even claimed she is doomed to haunt the castle until the treasure is found.[6]

Over the subsequent centuries there have been numerous sightings of the 'White Lady' walking the castle grounds. In *Ghosts of Old England* (1987) Terence Whitaker relates an account of a disturbing incident that took place during the eighteenth century when the castle was in a dilapidated state and only an estate labourer and his family occupied a few habitable rooms. The parents slept in one room, the children in the other. One night the mother and father were awakened by the screams of one of their children. They rushed to the children's bedroom to find one of them sitting up in bed, screaming, 'White Lady! White Lady!' Both parents checked around the room and found nothing untoward and reassured the child that he had suffered a nightmare. The boy said:

> She's gone and she looked angry at me because I would not go with her. She was a fine lady and she sat at my bedside, wringing her hands and crying hard. She then kissed me and she sat at my bedside and asked me to go with her and she would make me rich, as she had buried a large box of gold, many hundreds of years since and she would give it to me, because she could not rest as long as it was there. I told her I was scared and she said she would carry me, and lifting me up, I cried out. This frightened her away.[7]

The boy did settle down again, only for the same thing to occur on the following three nights. The parents removed him to sleep elsewhere and that seems to have ended the nocturnal visitations but after these incidents the boy would never enter any part of the old castle alone, even in daylight.

Bolton Castle, Wensleydale, Yorkshire

Bolton Castle was built by Sir Richard le Scrope, Lord Chancellor of England to Richard II, and took from 1378 to 1399 to build. The sixteenth-century writer John Leland described the castle as having 'An Astronomical Clock' in the courtyard and described how smoke was conveyed from the hearth in the hall through tunnels.

Mary, Queen of Scots was first imprisoned in Bolton Castle for six months but managed to escape. She managed to raise forces, and went into battle against the English at the Battle of Langside in 1568 but were defeated and Mary was taken prisoner. She was initially held at Carlisle Castle, which proved unsuitable. She was moved to Bolton Castle in July 1568. At this time her keeper was Sir Francis Knollys who in appraising the security of the fortress wrote:

> This howse appeareth to be very strong, very fayre, and very stately after the olde manner of building, and is the highest walled house I have seen, and has but one entrance thereinto.

Mary was given owner Henry Scrope's own apartments in the south-west tower for her accommodation and she was far from alone. Her retinue of fifty-one gentlemen, servants and ladies-in-waiting came with her and thirty of them were accommodated in the castle, while the rest found lodgings nearby. Mary did not give a favourable account of her captivity at Bolton Castle, which she described as cold and damp. Her ghost is said to walk around the courtyard, which is not surprising as the potato-garden in which she took exercise was described by her as 'fitter to keep pigs in than to bear the name of a garden'. Mary was removed from Bolton Castle for the last time in January 1569 and was taken Tutbury in Staffordshire where she would spend most of the next eighteen years before she was finally executed in 1587.

A visitor to Bolton Castle in 1878 claimed to have seen the ghost of Mary, Queen of Scots quite clearly. Initially thinking it was the farmer's wife, yet her apparel was so different and her countenance so noble, that she just looked from another age. The visitor said:

> I ran after her and was going to touch her when she turned round and I saw her face. It was very lovely. Her dress seemed to be made of black velvet. After looking at me for a moment she went on and disappeared through the door leading to the winding stone staircase in the angle turret of the west tower.

Cawood Castle, Cawood, Selby, Yorkshire

A story recorded in John Aubrey's *Miscellanies* (1696) tells of how a ghost revealed a murder. The tale begins on Monday 14 April 1690, when William Barwick went for a stroll with his wife Mary to the grounds of Cawood Castle.

Mary was pregnant and was not far off full term; it should have been a special time together. William told her to walk before him as they crossed the narrow bridge over Bishop's Dyke and made their way to the pond surrounded by thick rushes when suddenly he seized Mary and threw her into the pond, and did not let go his hold till she was drowned and her life was extinct. William would never explain why he did this. He then pulled Mary's body out of the water and concealed it among the rushes and returned home. At dusk he returned with a spade, dug a hole by the side of the pond and buried his wife. He then went to his brother-in-law, Thomas Lofthouse, and informed him that Mary had gone to stay with their uncle in Selby.

On the following Tuesday Lofthouse, who lived near that same pond, went there to fill his pail to water his hedge. There he saw a woman walking in front of him wearing a brown dress and a white hood. It was just the sort of clothes Mary would wear; in fact, she looked very much like her. The woman sat down by the pond on a small green mound. Lofthouse walked by her and as he filled his pail, he looked at her face. It was very pale 'and her teeth were visible' but he was convinced its visage was that of Mary, his wife's sister. The woman he saw was also 'dandling something like a white bag on her lap evidently suggestive, indeed, of her unborn babe that was slain with her'.[8]

They did not speak; something just felt very wrong. Mr Lofthouse was troubled by what he had seen but he did not mention it until after his family duty of prayers had been completed. The thoughts of apparition had become so overpowering he told his wife what he had seen, 'who laying the whole circumstances together, immediately inferred that her sister was either drowned or otherwise murdered'.

Lofthouse went to see the uncle in York the following day where Mary was supposed to be, but he had not seen Mary, nor was he expecting her. Lofthouse obtained a warrant for Barwick's arrest, but Barwick denied everything and went on to claim he had sold his wife. Such a thing was not unknown in the seventeenth century, but suspicions were aroused when he could not say to whom or where he transacted the deal. When the pond was searched, Mary's shallow grave was found and her body was uncovered. Barwick confessed to her murder, was duly tried, found guilty and hanged.[9] Mary was given a Christian burial but sadly it seems her ghost cannot rest and she is still occasionally seen near the pond and around the castle.

Chillingham Castle, Chillingham, Northumberland

Chillingham began as a monastery in the late twelfth century. In 1298 King Edward I, 'Longshanks', the man who became known as 'The Hammer of the Scots', stayed there when on his way to Scotland to do battle with a Scottish army led by William Wallace, 'Braveheart'. Fortified as a castle in 1344. Chillingham was regularly used as a staging post for English armies as they advanced to Scotland and was subject to attacks by the Scots too. In 1513 it was attacked by an invading Scottish army under James IV and survived a serious assault during the 'Pilgrimage of Grace' in 1536, but it never fell to an attacking enemy. The castle was the seat of the earls of Tankerville for centuries and is currently the home of Sir Humphry Wakefield, 2nd Baronet.

Chillingham Castle is claimed to be Britain's most haunted historic castle. It has been the author's pleasure to investigate the hauntings there with some of the world's best-known paranormal investigators including Dave Schrader and Sam and Colby. The figure that has become known at the castle as John 'Dragfoot' Sage, the man said to have acted as torturer for King Edward I, is problematic because there is no historical evidence he ever existed. He has made himself known to reputable paranormal investigators and mediums and has even interacted with them. He is often described as 'a dark entity' and that is exactly what I think it is. John Sage is a construct, an entity that has latched on to the name and feeds on the fear and reactions of those it can reach. Be very careful of that one, folks. The idea of a dark entity being at large is no joke either. George Montagu Bennet, 7th Earl of Tankerville, even hired none other than Aleister Crowley, one of the infamous occultists of the day to protect him from witchcraft in the early twentieth century.

That said, there is a host of presences and spirits in the walls of the ancient castle. In my quest to uncover some of the earliest accounts of the hauntings I have found references in newspapers during the nineteenth century to a ghost described as a 'Radiant Boy' appearing in a bed chamber at Chillingham Castle, but they were best documented by Leonora Countess Tankerville, who wrote in 1926:

> Perhaps our principal and most famous apparition was known as the 'Radiant Boy,' which used to be seen in what is now called the Pink Room. There, when from the Clock Tower the hour of midnight sounded, were heard the cries and moans of a child in pain and in an agony of fear. Always the noises came from a spot nearest to a passage cut through the ten feet thick wall into the adjoining tower; and, as the blood-curdling cries died slowly away a bright halo of light began to form close to the old four-poster bed. Anyone sleeping there saw, gently approaching them, the figure of a young boy dressed in blue, and surrounded by the light. It was in the adjoining Tower that the bones of a boy of tender years, and some fragments of a blue dress were later discovered. These poor remains were reverently removed and decently interred in consecrated ground, since when the figure has never been seen again.[10]

That said, they may not have found and buried all the boy's bones as Sir Humphrey recalls friends staying in that room told him that there must be an electrical fault in the wall since a blue flash woke them up during the night … but here are no electrics in that wall. The countess continued:

> Our next best-known and authenticated ghost is that of Lady Mary Berkeley, wife of Ford, Lord Grey of Wark and Chillingham and Earl of Tankerville, who looks for her errant husband. That gentleman ran away with her own sister, Lady Henrietta, thus giving rise to great scandal and a lawsuit tried before the famous – or shall we say infamous? – Judge Jeffreys in the reign of King Charles II. … The end of it all was a heartless desertion; the poor lady was left in her dark and lovely Castle with only a fatherless baby girl as her companion. To this day the rustle of her dress is sometimes heard along the corridors and stairs, and as the disappointed and anxious wraith passes by, a chill, as of cold air, seems to sweep through one's very marrow.[11]

In another account the countess related another story about the painting:

> Less sad, but still interesting, was a rather remarkable episode a few years back in connection with a family portrait which was said to walk. Not only had our own nursery been disturbed by the restlessness of this picture but the children of friends, and their nurse, declared that she stepped out of her frame and frightened them by following them about. When, soon after, a well-known psychologist [Robert King] came as a guest, my husband told him this story, and he asked to be taken there after everyone had gone to bed. Late that night they went over to where the picture used to hang and he sat for a couple of hours waiting for Her Ladyship to appear, his host being in the next room meanwhile. As they came out, he was laughingly asked if he had seen anything. 'Nothing malefic,' was his reply, and that seemed final. But the following morning, while going through the rooms he paused before an oil painting and exclaimed, 'That is the woman I saw last night!' This puzzled Lord Tankerville and he replied, 'It is not the one who is said to walk.' 'Well,' answered his guest, 'that is the one I saw.'

Later in the same day my husband spoke of it to his old nurse who is still with us, and she at once explained, 'Oh, m'Lord, don't you know? That is a portrait of the same lady, only done when she was much older.'

The countess also recounts the story of one of the most enigmatic hauntings in the castle:

> In what is called 'the inner pantry' there has been seen a frail figure in white. This was where the silver in use was stored, during my father-in-law's lifetime. A footman had to sleep there to safeguard it. One night he had turned in when he was accosted by a lady in white, very pale, who asked him for a glass of water. Thinking for the moment it was one of the visitors he turned away to obey her behest, when he suddenly remembered that he was locked in and no visitor could possibly have entered. On turning round, he found the figure had vanished. This same figure was seen also by a guest who made notes of her psychic experiences in the various rooms of the Castle without anything having been told her beforehand; I was rather surprised to see that she alluded to the longing for water of a female ghost who 'must have been slowly poisoned in olden times'.

The countess did not just hear of and see phantoms around the castle; she may have witnessed 'time slips' too:

> I had a remarkable experience one day just before the Great War, when there was so much occult disturbance of every kind. One eventide, after an exceptionally busy time, I sat down for a few moments' rest in a room facing the Cheviot Hills. Very soon I could not help noticing that the gale sounded in the wide old chimney like the distant boom of cannon, and as I looked out on the usually restful formal garden there, too, waving branches and heavy drifting clouds assumed a menacing and warlike aspect.
>
> As I looked, the form of a woman seemed to take shape before me, walking on the parapet of a tower apparently

> as solid as that wherein I sat. She was in the garb of a Dominican Abbess, and after looking eagerly towards the hills of Scotland she knelt beside the battlements as if in prayer. A man stood beside her proudly erect, handsome and richly dressed; he, too, was scanning the horizon towards the enemy country.
>
> A few paces behind were two men in velvet court dress of the time of King Henry VIII. They were chatting in subdued tones. In the background, on the farther parapet, a halberdier paced up and down on sentry duty. I got up to watch the scene from the window, thinking I was about to witness some tragedy of former times.
>
> Presently I called to my son in the next room, but he was out; then a housemaid came in to close the shutters and asked a couple of questions. I thought, surely it will have disappeared – but no! I saw another woman bringing the Abbess an ermine cape, and the man's rich dress was covered now by a surcoat. The atmosphere was tense: with a feeling of impending danger, of fighting about to begin! I spoke to them twice, and asked if I could be of any service, when the man who was now pacing back stopped and looked at me was the face of my husband but in the garb of France four centuries ago! Then, who was the Abbess? Was that myself and why the anxiety? What was about to happen? If it was me, what was I praying God to avert? It was not long before we knew, not long before the din of battle sounded in our twentieth century ears and official directions were sent to us in case of an invasion! I had inadvertently 'tuned in' as it were to a similar moment long ago.[12]

In another article it revealed the countess had another possible time slip or witnessed a residual manifestation before the outbreak of the Great War:

> she seemed to see a group of figures on the battlements, of a period before the union of Scotland and England. The figures seemed to be looking apprehensively to the horizon in the direction of Scotland, as if expecting a raid. This incident

> suggested that there was some kind of registration or record of events which in special circumstances could be sensed again.[13]

The countess continued to encounter the ghosts at Chillingham Castle over the years she was there; in 1935 she gave a talk at the Edinburgh Psychic College and spoke of:

> When she slept on the east side of the castle, in what was called the audit room, an old woman with a lamp used to come to the bedside, peering at her. Her children often spoke of a room at the north side as having in it a 'black thing'.[14]

The latter, considering the possibility there is dark entity in the castle, is particularly disturbing, and even Sir Humphrey had to admit: 'We got the place exorcised some years back, but the priest said he couldn't shift the spirits.'[15]

Chipchase Castle, near Wark, Northumberland

The Chipchase Castle we see today is a fine fourteenth-century tower house with a mansion alongside built by Cuthbert Heron in 1621 that is quite simply one of finest examples of Jacobean architecture in the country. In a feature for Newcastle's *Sunday Sun* newspaper in October 1937, feature writer Dorothy Whitfield revealed the problem Chipchase Castle had in retaining staff:

> There are servant problems – and servant problems – Miss Marjorie Taylor, chatelaine for Chipchase Castle, for her father Alderman Tom Taylor since her mother's death last year, has a servant problem that is not unique among the stately old homes Northumberland: Ghosts! 'We dare not encourage belief in the old ghost story of Chipchase,' she told me when I called on her last week. 'If we did, we would never keep a servant.' It is a pity for the sinister old pele tower is a perfect setting with a spiral staircase of sixty-five stone steps worn from the tread of centuries which for so

> long was the grim home of lawless and quick-tempered barons of old Northumberland.
>
> Unlike most ghosts the Chipchase ghost has a name. He was one Sir Reginald Fitz-Urse so tradition has it, who was starved to death in one of the great prison chambers of the tower and afterwards haunted the scene of his suffering, startling passers [-by with sounds of] faint-clank armour and the eerie groans of a dying man. … He has a companion, an unnamed, who is said to have been killed in one of the wall chambers of the tower where he vainly sought refuge from a murderous band in pursuit of him.

The groans and clanks of Sir Reginald and the spectral wanderings of the murdered man in the wall are still claimed to be occasionally heard.

Dunstanburgh Castle, Embleton, Northumberland

The two gaunt, ruined towers of Dunstanburgh Castle have been a distinctive feature of the Northumberland coast for centuries. The original castle was built in 1313 by Thomas, Earl of Lancaster, a cousin of King Edward II. The castle passed to John of Gaunt in the 1380s who upgraded the fortifications, and it became his power base as Lieutenant of the Scottish Marches. During the Wars of the Roses the castle sided with the House of Lancaster, but was compelled to submit to the Yorkists in 1461. Its joint constable, Sir Ralph Percy, declared for Lancaster again the following year. In June 1464 the Yorkists finally secured the castle and it was left to ruin.

The haunting of Dunstanburgh Castle goes all the way back to Thomas Plantagenet, Earl of Lancaster, the man who built it, who in his day was one of the most powerful men in England. Thomas led a rebellion against the king but was defeated at the Battle of Boroughbridge on 16 March 1322. He was captured, tried and found guilty of treason at Pontefract Castle. Sentenced to death, on 22 March 1322 he was beheaded on the hill north of St John's Priory … eventually. It took the executioner eleven blows to finally sever Thomas's head from his body. The earl's decapitated ghost is said to haunt Dunstanburgh Castle carrying his mangled head that still bears the expression of acute pain and the anguish it bore as he died.

Featherstone Castle, near Haltwhistle, Northumberland

Featherstone Castle is a fortified manor house dating back to the fourteenth century that has been in the Featherstonehaugh family for centuries. The castle looks every bit the setting for a great gothic horror novel and there is a suitably dramatic ghost story associated with it. The following account is based on versions of the tale published in the nineteenth century that set it during the seventeenth century: Abigail Featherstonehaugh was the one and only child of the then owner of Featherstone Castle, and her father was determined that his daughter, sole heiress of the line, must marry the husband that *he* thought best.

The fair Abigail, however, had made her own choice, and the man she wished to marry was bold Ridley of Hardriding. The problem was that a feud existed between their families, a feud like many in the land of the Border Reivers that had gone on so long it had been forgotten what it was really about, but the hatred remained only too real and when Ridley asked her father for her hand in marriage, he would not give his consent. Abigail wept and pleaded with her father, but he would not countenance the union. Instead, a marriage was arranged for her with a suitable son of another wealthy family he did approve of.

The day of the wedding was set for 17 January and after the service the newly married couple set off with their wedding party to ride the bounds of the estate. As the evening shadows began to close in and the party was returning to the castle through the romantic glen known as Pynkinscleugh, they came across bold Ridley and his men who had been lying in wait for them. He attempted to carry her off but in the ensuing struggle she caught a fatal thrust from a sword which pierced her heart, killing her on the spot. Mad with grief, Ridley declared that none should be spared and ordered the whole retinue to be wiped out.

Meanwhile, back at the castle, Abigail's father knew nothing of what had happened. The afternoon came and went, the feast was laid, with minstrels in attendance, and a throng of guests arrived eager to begin the festivities, but there was no sign of the wedding party. Dusk turned to night and still the bridal party had not returned. The food grew cold, the music ended early and the guests were asked to leave and Abigail's father sat in his chair by the fire and gazed into the flames.

As the clock chimed the midnight hour, the sound of hooves broke the tense silence in the castle and Baron Featherstonehaugh looked up expecting to see a happy but tired return of the group … but into the hall rode the bridal party and every man and woman of it was ashen faced and ghastly, many of them livid with streaks of blood or great, gaping wounds. The features of some were painfully distorted, as if they had died in great agony and all their eyes were wide open, with a cold, glassy stare that was horrid to behold as they rode slowly through the furniture as if it was not there.

The old baron was struck rigid with fear and disbelief as the realisation and full horror of what he was seeing hit him. A cold wind suddenly blew through the hall, the candles guttered and, in an instant, the ghostly marriage party disappeared and all that was left was an occasional crackle of the dying embers of the fire. It was too much for the old baron to take and he went mad and died not long afterwards. Every year on the anniversary of these terrible events the ghostly wedding party is claimed to ride through the wooded pass at Pynkinscleugh where the dreadful slaughter took place.

Haughton Castle, near Humshaugh, Northumberland

Haughton Castle is a private home and not open to the public. It began as a thirteenth-century tower house and was enlarged and fortified in the fourteenth century by the Widdrington family.

The following account is an edited version of 'The Castle Spectre: A Legend of Haughton' published in the *Newcastle Chronicle* in December 1893:

> Haughton Castle, situated on the North Tyne, is reputed to have a spectre of its own, said to have been the ghost of one of those daring mosstroopers who made life and property on the Borders unsafe. The story goes that in the reign of Henry VIII when Lord Dacre of Gilsland was Warden of the Middle Marches, a loud complaint arose in the Northern Counties on account of his being more than suspected of taking bribes, directly or indirectly, from the more influential of those freebooters, such as the chiefs of the clans Armstrong, Elliot, Scott, Kerr and Graeme.
>
> The fact was, that during a great part of his wardenship, the mosstroopers, especially those of the Scottish side and

the Debatable Land, were more troublesome than they had ever been before. No man's horses or cattle were safe unless he submitted to the ignominy of paying blackmail to some notable hard-riding chieftain.

The Lord of Haughton Castle, Sir John de Widdrington, was one of the most energetic men in this movement for the redress of grievances. He is reported to have been a learned and clerkly man, and as gallant a knight as any in the whole North Country. His bravery was noted at the Battle of Otterburn in the ballad of *Chevy Chase* for it was he, for whom the poet's

– heart was woe,
As one in doleful dumps;
For when his legs were smitten in two
He fought upon his stumps.

Sir John determined to lodge a formal complaint about Dacre to the Cardinal in York when his men managed to capture the leader of a gang of mosstroopers – no less a personage than Archie Armstrong, chief of the reiver Armstrongs. The prisoner was brought in triumph to Haughton, and safely lodged in the deep, dark, underground dungeon of the castle. Then, Sir John and a deputation set off for York and after two days' hard riding, they duly arrived at York, where they rested the third day and were to be presented to the cardinal on the fourth day.

On that morning, they were on their way to the Archiepiscopal Palace, when it all at once flashed across the Lord of Haughton's mind that he had quite forgotten, before leaving home, to give his servants any instructions as to how they should treat his prisoner, and he found likewise, to his utter consternation, that he had brought away with him the key of the dungeon, which he usually carried attached to his girdle. Being a truly humane man, as well as a firm supporter of law and order, he was horror-struck at the possible consequences of his neglect; for it was now the fourth day of Armstrong's confinement and during the whole of that time he could not have received either meat or drink.

Without waiting to see the cardinal, he turned that instant the face of his horse northward and galloped away as hard as he could – so hard that before he reached Durham, sixty-seven miles off, his horse dropped dead under him. To borrow another steed was the work of a few minutes; and this horse he urged to its utmost speed, so that by the middle of the night of the day on which he left York, he was thundering at the outer portal of his own castle. Soiled and stained with the mire of the roads he had traversed, his face flushed with a fearful excitement, and his voice nearly gone, he could only shout, on the gate being opened, in a hoarse, harsh, raucous tone, 'The prisoner.'

The domestic could only answer that they had heard nothing of him for the last four-and twenty hours, though before that he had been very noisy. 'Bring me a torch!' was his master's instant exclamation. The light was at once brought, the key was turned in the lock, the door was thrown open, grating on its rusty hinges, and Armstrong was found lying on the steps leading down into the gloomy vault, stark dead, either, starved to death or suffocated by foul air. In his mortal agony he had gnawed the flesh from one of his arms, and his features were contorted in such horrid fashion as to strike terror into those who looked on him.

How his mortal remains were disposed of we are not told but the spectre of the unhappy man haunted the castle. In the dead of night, shrieks of the most agonising kind were heard issuing from the dungeon, and piercing and resounding through every room in the place. The consequence was that no servant would stay within its precincts, and the family were at their wits' end how to get peace and rest nights. At length the Rector of Simonburn exorcised the ghost, by means, it is said, of black-lettered Bible and so long as the sacred volume remained in the castle, the ghost continued to be quiet but if the Bible was ever removed from the castle the horrifying shrieks and moans were sure to start again.[16]

Hylton Castle, Sunderland, County Durham

One of the classic haunted castle stories is 'The Cauld Lad of Hylton'. The following article from February 1890 delves into the tale:

> Formerly the homes of nearly every Scottish and of many English, families of importance were haunted by domestic spirits known as 'Brownies'. Hylton Castle was one of the most magnificent dwellings in the north of England, but now hastening to decay, and among other weird inhabitants was for a long while frequented by a Brownie, popularly known as the 'Cauld Lad of Hylton'.
>
> As a rule, these domestic spectres appear to take up their abode in any suitable dwelling without the usual precedent of a crime, as is the case with a ghost or apparition of the ordinary type, and to have generally employed themselves for the benefit of the household. The antiquary Surtees, in his History of Durham assumes the being that haunted Hylton Castle to have been one of these somewhat common place spirits, and although thereon other eerie stories of the Cauld Lad, it will be as well to give the historian's account first.
>
> The Cauld Lad, he says, was seldom seen, but was heard nightly by the servants, who slept in the great hall. If the kitchen were left in perfect order, they heard him amusing himself by breaking plates and dishes, hurling the pewter in all directions, and throwing everything into confusion. If, on the contrary, the apartment had been left in disarray, a practice which the servants found it most prudent to adopt, the indefatigable goblin arranged everything with the greatest precision.
>
> This poor spirit, whose pranks were never of a dangerous or hurtful character, was at length banished from haunts by the usual and universally known expedient of presenting him with a suit of clothes. A cloak and hood were laid before the fire, and the domestics sat up watching at a prudent distance. At 12 o'clock he glided gently in, stood by the glowing embers and eyed the garments provided him

very attentively, tried them on and, seemed delighted with his appearance in them, frisking about for some time and cutting several somersaults until on hearing the first cock-crow, he twitched his mantle about him and disappeared with the malediction usually adopted on occasions:

Here's a cloak, and here's a hood,
The Cauld Lad o' Hylton will do no more good.

Although this spirit was thus summarily disposed of by the historian, the inhabitants of Hilton and its vicinity for many generations continued to believe in its frequent reappearance, and over the glowing embers told wonderful tales of its deeds. So strange were its doings at times, and so frequent its apparition, that it was difficult to retain the domestics in the castle.

Among other stories that told of the terror contrived to imbue the minds of the servants is one of a dairymaid who was too fond of helping herself to the richest cream the pantry afforded. One day, as this not over scrupulous young woman was taking her usual sips from the various pans, the Cauld Lad suddenly addressed her from some invisible vantage ground, 'Ye taste, and ye taste, and ye taste, but ye never gie the Cauld Lad a taste!' Hearing this appalling accusation, the affrighted maid dropped the spoon on the ground, rushed out of the place, and could never be induced to enter it again.

The local tradition of the Cauld Lad more closely assimilates his nature to that of any ordinary ghost or apparition, and in no way to the Brownie of our forefathers. The popular idea is that a lad, a domestic of the house, was cruelly ill-treated and kept confined in a cupboard … He is supposed to have received the suggestively awesome name of the Cauld Lad from his stiff and stark form having been discovered in the pond.

Robert Surtees, the Durham antiquarian, endeavours to explain the origin of this ancient legend by reference to a murder of Roger Skelton, apparently a servant, by his master,

> Robert Hylton, of Hylton, on 3 July 1609. Hylton was found guilty of having killed Skelton but received a pardon some few months after conviction. According to the old tale, the lord of Hylton one day, in a wrath or intemperance, enraged at the delay in bringing his horse after he had ordered it, rushed to the stable, and finding the boy, whose duty it was to have brought the horse, loitering about, he seized a hay-fork, and struck him with it. Intentionally or not, he had given the lad a mortal blow. The tale proceeds to tell how the murderer covered the victim with straw until night-time, when he took the body and flung it into the pond, where the skeleton was discovered in the last Lord of Hylton's time.[17]

Lieutenant-Colonel Briggs, who lived in Hylton Castle, told the Newcastle Society of Antiquaries during their visit there in 1887 how 'the story of the Cauld Lad and his haunting of the castle, is still firmly believed in by many of the people in the district'.[18] The folk tradition is the 'Cauld Lad' sings the following song of how long he expects it will be before his ghost will finally be laid or exorcised:

Wae's me, wae's me,
The acorn's not yet fallen from the tree,
That's to grow the wood,
That's to make the cradle,
That's to rock the bairn,
That's to grow to the man
That's to lay me.

Raby Castle, near Staindrop, County Durham

Raby Castle is a private home, but it is opened to the public seasonally. The castle was probably built on the site of an earlier house built by the Neville family who have held the manor since the thirteenth century. The current castle was built between 1367 and 1390. It would be at Raby that Charles Neville, 6th Earl of Westmorland planned the 'Rising in the North' with the Percy family in 1569. Their aim was to remove Elizabeth I from the throne and replace her with her Catholic cousin,

Mary, Queen of Scots. The rising failed and Raby Castle was confiscated by the Crown. The ghostly spectre of Charles Neville appears on the stairs and still lingers in the Barons' Hall to this day.

His ghost is not the only one to haunt Raby Castle. A ghostly man rides a horse around the grounds and disappears near the gatehouse. A horse has been seen in the grounds.

Central to the story are Christopher Vane, 1st Baron Barnard of Raby Castle (1653–1723), a quiet man who loved his books, and his wife, the formidable Lady Elizabeth Holles (1657–1725), eldest daughter of the Earl of Clare, a woman with a reputation for having an 'ungovernable temper'. When their eldest son, Gilbert, told his parents that he intended to marry Mary, the daughter of Guildford MP Morgan Randyll, in 1714, they were not happy. Or rather Elizabeth was not happy; she was very much of the opinion that Gilbert should only marry a lady of aristocratic blood – anyone less and he would be 'marrying beneath himself'.

Gilbert would not be dissuaded; his parents could not stop him, so they set about the destruction of his inheritance at Raby Castle instead. Two hundred workmen were employed to strip the castle of its lead, glass, doors and furnishings. Household goods were sold for a pittance or burned on a huge bonfire, most of the fine woodlands were cut down and many of the deer in the park were slaughtered.

Gilbert successfully sued his parents in the Court of Chancery. They were ordered to cease the destruction, and a rebuilding programme began. And what for? Gilbert and Mary remained happily married but the bitter anger of Lady Elizabeth never seems to have been appeased, and it was never forgotten by locals who dubbed her 'The Old Hell Cat'.

The ghost of Christopher Vane wisely enjoys haunting his library of beloved books while the ghost of Lady Elizabeth is said to sweep through the corridors of the castle 'like a galleon in full sail'. Those who have seen her face describe it as 'very old looking with wild eyes that glow in the dark'. She is also said to haunt the battlements where she seethes and paces back and forth as she knits away furiously with red-hot needles.

Scarborough Castle, Scarborough, Yorkshire

The ruins of Scarborough Castle high on the rock headland still have a remarkably commanding presence over the seaside town. The castle began as a great tower built by William le Gros, Count of Aumâle, in the twelfth century. It acceded to the Crown a few years later. Henry II began the development of the castle and over the next hundred years successive monarchs turned it into one of the greatest royal fortresses in England.

In early May 1312 one of King Edward II's favourites, Piers Gaveston, Earl of Cornwall took refuge in Scarborough Castle from the forces of the rebellious Barons Pembroke, de Warenne, Percy and Clifford, who laid siege to the castle. On 19 May 1312 Gaveston negotiated what he believed to be an end of the siege with an agreed safe conduct to York, where the barons could meet with the king. What happened, however, was Gaveston was arrested and taken to Warwick where he was condemned to death before an assembly of barons 'for violating the terms of the Ordinances'. On 19 June, he was taken out on the road towards Kenilworth as far as Blacklow Hill where he was run through with a sword and beheaded.

Gaveston's headless ghost returned to haunt the ruins of Scarborough Castle. His ghost seems to be an angry one and has even been known to rush at anyone wandering around the castle at night to drive them to over the battlements to take a fatal plummet.

Skipsea Castle, Skipsea Brough, Driffield, Yorkshire

Skipsea Castle could easily be missed today but this earthwork should not be missed for it dates from before 1086 and is all that remains of one of the first Norman motte-and-bailey castles to be raised in Yorkshire. It also has one of the oldest recorded hauntings of a 'white lady' ghost. The story is recorded in one of the first popular ghost books, *The Haunted Homes and Family Traditions of Great Britain*, by John Henry Ingram, first published in 1897. I was fortunate to obtain a copy of this book over thirty years ago when I was at college from David Ferrow, the much-missed antiquarian book dealer in Great Yarmouth. It is one of the volumes that has a real aura of mystique about it; with a lovely, decorative binding, it exudes the atmosphere that within it are old ghost stories of good import. Here is the story of the haunting at Skipsea Castle from that very volume that I bought all those years ago. If you have not read it before, I hope you will enjoy it as much as I did:

Skipsea, an out of the way Yorkshire village, on the sea-coast between Bridlington and Hornsea, is celebrated for one of the most enduring apparitions on record. 'The White Lady of Skipsea', as this phantom is styled, has haunted the old castle, of which, now-a-days, little more than the foundations remain, ever since the days of William the Conqueror.

This Skipsea ghost, whose local habitation no native of the place would venture near after nightfall, is described as haunting the Castle mound, and its vicinity, in the form of a beautiful young woman, of mournful aspect, attired in long white drapery. Occasionally she may be seen flitting about the intrenchments or slopes of the Castle mound, and at times, even in the daylight, she is seen wandering about the precincts of what was formerly her home. No ill effects are reported to follow the appearance of this apparition, whose story is detailed by Mr F. Ross in his interesting 'Yorkshire Legends and Traditions' now appearing in the Leeds Mercury, in these words: –

The White Lady was the wife of Drogo de Bevere, a Flemish soldier of fortune, who took up arms under the banner of the Norman Duke William, in the army he assembled together for the conquest of England. He was a good and valiant soldier, and fought with great bravery at the battle of Hastings, for which he was rewarded by Duke William, when he had subdued Northumbria, with a grant of the district of Holderness, which he constituted a Seigniory, and made Drogo the first Lord, who went to reside there, and erected a castle at Skipsea, as a defence against the Danes, who were wont to land at Flamborough, and to serve as his caput baronium, where he exercised a semi-regal rule over the district.

Although a brave warrior, he was tyrannical and oppressive to the Angles and Danes of Holderness, whose lands had been reft from them in his behoof, and whom he reduced to complete serfdom. He was subject to ungovernable bursts of passion, and, when in this mood, would perpetrate the grossest acts of cruelty and injustice. He was also exceedingly covetous and avaricious, as was evidenced by his seizure, by forcible means, of the lands in Holderness belonging to St John's Church, at Beverley, which had been specially confirmed to the Canons, by King William; but these he was compelled to disgorge.

As a further proof of his favour the Conqueror gave him one of his nieces in marriage, whose identity has not been clearly ascertained, but who, possibly, from the obscurity in which she is enveloped, may have been a grand-daughter of William's mother, Herteva, by her second marriage. However this may be, they were married, and he carried her down to his Yorkshire domain, where they resided together in Skipsea Castle. The marriage does not appear to have been a happy one; their tempers were incompatible. He was brutal in his tastes and manners, delighting only in war, the chase, and tyrannising over his menials and tenants; she, gentle and refined, as were the Norman ladies of the period. He always treated her with churlishness, often with savage barbarity, frequently threatened her with death, and, at length, in a fit of fierce passion, caused her to be poisoned.

The deed was no sooner perpetrated than Drogo perceived his folly, feeling assured that her uncle would take vengeance upon him for it, and that the result would be a confiscation of the Seigniory, and his execution as a murderer. His craft and subtlety, however, served him well in this crisis. His victim was scarcely cold when he mounted the fleetest horse in his stable and rode southwards, bating neither whip nor spur until he reached the Court of the King. He represented to the latter that he was very desirous of taking his wife across sea to Flanders, to show her the land of his birth, and introduce her to his family.

The King applauded the idea, and granted his permission for them to leave England, upon which Drogo represented that the domain which had been given him was of so poor a nature that it would grow nothing but oats, and that a great portion of it consisted but of woodland and morass, so that he was utterly destitute of the means of taking shipping to cross the sea. 'If that be all,' said the King, 'you shall not be baulked of your pleasure trip, for want of money,' and he gave him an order on his exchequer for a sum sufficient for the purpose.

As soon as he got the money, he took leave of the King, hastened to the sea-side, and set sail for Flanders. He had not been long gone, when a messenger arrived from Skipsea, who informed the King of the death of his niece and the manner of it. Upon receipt of this intelligence the King sent a body of horsemen after the murderer, with instructions to bring him back, alive or dead. But Drogo had got too much start, and eluded the pursuit, arriving in due course in Flanders, but what was his after-fate records tell not.

We have no account of the place of burial of the unfortunate lady. There was no church at Skipsea at the time of the Domesday survey, but we find that Stephen, Earle of Albemarle, Lord of the Seigniory in the time of Rufus, gave his church of the Castle of Skipsea to the Monastery of Albemarle, and it is probable that within its walls her body was deposited. Her spirit, however, seems not to have found a resting place, but for the past eight hundred years has been wandering about the scene of her unhappy wifehood. The phantom has not appeared in recent years, but in the Hull Advertiser, early in the present century, we have an account of the apparition having been seen. The editor prefaces the account by saying – 'In introducing the following singular article, it may be necessary to state that the writer as well as the two persons upon whose testimony the circumstances rest, are well known to us, and above all suspicion of having thus related anything save what they believed to be strictly correct.'

The writer states that he was visiting a lady in Holderness, when the conversation of the party then assembled turned upon supernatural appearances, the lady expressing the opinion that they 'were owing to some misapprehension of the senses', upon which a gentleman of the party, of unimpeachable character, said that he was under the necessity of differing from the lady. 'For,' said he, 'about ten years ago I was travelling on horseback one afternoon from Bridlington to Hornsea, and just as I was descending the brow of a hill, on the south of Skipsea, I observed a woman, apparently young, dressed in white, walking a little before me on my left hand, between the hedge and the road. Supposing that she had been visiting at a house on the top of the hill, I turned my head to see if there were any persons in attendance at the door, but the door was shut and none to be seen.

'My curiosity being now greater than before to know who this genteel person was, I followed her at the distance of twenty or thirty yards down the hill, which was 100 or 150 yards long, and expected when she got to the bottom, where there was a small brook, that I should meet her in attempting to gain the carriage bridge, but to my great astonishment, when she approached the brook, instead of turning to the right to gain the bridge, she vanished from my sight, at the very time that my eyes were fixed upon her. As soon as I got home, I related the strange affair to my family; and as it was light, and I had not previously been thinking about apparitions, nor was I ever in the habit of speculating on such subjects, I am firmly persuaded that what I saw was one.'

The lady of the house said that the recital had made 'a greater impression on her than anything she had ever heard before. 'For,' continued she, 'about five years ago I had a servant, who was a young man of good character and of a bold, active disposition, one who professed a disregard for any extraordinary appearances. In the month of November, about Martinmas time, he requested leave to go to Bridlington and also to be accommodated with a horse, which was granted him. Being very desirous to make a long holiday of it, he rose early in the morning and set off two hours before daybreak; but, to our very great surprise, returned home early in the afternoon, before it was dark.

'On being questioned if anything was the matter with him, he replied that he had been so much alarmed that he was resolved never to travel alone in the dark if he could avoid it.' 'For, as I was cantering along Skipsea Lane in the morning, bending forward with my face downwards, the horse suddenly bolted from the road to such a distance that I was very nearly dismounted. On recovering myself and looking about to discover what had frightened my horse, I saw a fine lady, dressed in white, with something like a black veil over her head, standing close by. How I got to Skipsea I cannot tell, but I was so frightened that I durst go no farther but walked up and down the hill till it was light, when I found some persons going the same road, whom I accompanied to Bridlington.'

Chapter 3
The Midlands

Could it be so, that the ghost of Katherine was permitted to roam over those old precincts – making night hideous – and to fill with awe those who had been guilty of robbing the dead!
Frederick Simmons

Astley Castle, Astley, Warwickshire

Asley Castle was a fortified manor house that had been in the hands of the Astley family from the twelfth century. The castle passed by marriage to Reginald Grey, 3rd Baron Grey de Ruthyn in 1415. The Greys had acquired their status and power over the years as marcher lords who controlled the borderlands between England and Wales and by strategic marriages. The Greys rebuilt the castle in 1555, and the ruins left today mostly date from that time.

During the Grey family tenure in the fifteenth and sixteenth centuries, Astley Castle became a hub of national events. The daughter of Henry Grey, Duke of Suffolk and Elizabeth of York, Lady Jane Grey, was proclaimed queen in 1553. Her cousin Mary, the half-sister of the deceased king, had other ideas, drummed up supporters and took the crown. She would not be known as 'Bloody Mary' for no good reason. Mary would ensure the Greys were punished as a warning to all. Lady Jane, her husband and her father would all end up in the Tower of London, all three would be beheaded in February 1554 and Astley Castle was forfeited to the Crown.

Over the years after his execution the headless ghost of Henry Grey, Duke of Suffolk was said to have been seen around his old home. Henry's head was rediscovered in 1851 in the vault of Church of Holy Trinity, Minories, in the City of London. It was in a remarkable state of preservation having been packed into its casket with the oak sawdust from the scaffold. The blows from the axe were still easily discerned upon his neck.

Astley Castle eventually became a hotel in the 1960s but suffered a disastrous fire in 1978. After years as an overgrown ruin the castle has recently been preserved and even modern accommodations built into it. It is only accessible on designated open days.

Bolingbroke Castle, Bolingbroke, Lincolnshire

The ruins consisting of low walls and earthworks of what was the magnificent Bolingbroke Castle lie in a valley where the wolds rise out of the eastern Lincolnshire fens. Originally built by Ranulf de Blundeville, Earl of Chester and Lincoln, in the 1220s after his return from the Crusades, the castle was built in Spilsby greenstone, with five towers, a twin-towered gatehouse linked by a 16-feet-thick curtain wall to form an irregular polygonal enclosure, surrounded by a moat.

The castle passed by marriage to John of Gaunt (third son of King Edward III) who lived there with his wife Blanche of Lancaster (the daughter of Henry, Duke of Lancaster). While at the castle their son Henry of Bolingbroke was born in 1367. His cousin, King Richard II, was unpopular and Henry was encouraged to claim the throne of England in his stead. This was achieved quite deftly, on 1 October 1399. Richard was formally deposed and on 13 October, the feast day of Edward the Confessor, Henry was crowned King Henry IV.

From the fifteenth century to the early seventeenth century Bolingbroke Castle was used primarily as an administrative centre for the estates of the Duchy of Lancaster. It was during this latter period that Gervase Holles wrote the earliest known account of a most unusual haunting at Bolingbroke Castle in his *Lincolnshire Church Notes*, which he made between the years 1634–42 at the time when Sir William Mounson, Lord Castlemayne was constable of the castle:

> One thing is not to be passed by, affirmed as a certaine truth by many of ye inhabitants of ye towne upon their owne knowledge, which is, that ye castle is haunted by a certaine

> spirit in ye likenesse of a Hare; which att the meeting of ye Auditors doth usually runne betweene their legs, & sometymes overthrows them, & so passes away. They have pursued it doune into ye Castle yard, & seene it take in att a grate into a low cellar, & have followed it thither with a light, where notwithstanding that they did most narrowly observe it (& that there was noe other passage out, but by the doore or windowe, ye roome being all close framed of stones within, not having the least chinke or crevice,) yet they could never fynde it. And att other tymes it hath bin seene to run in at Iron-grates below into other of ye Grotto's (as there be many of them) & they have watched the place, & sent for Houndes, & put in after it; but after a while they have come crying out.[1]

Country folklore tells of how witches can turn themselves into hares; the persecution and fear of witches was already well known in Lincolnshire and across East Anglia at the time and many local people were in no doubt that the phantom hare was in fact the familiar or spirit of a witch who had returned to harass the castle administrators or perhaps had even brought a curse upon the castle. In less than a year of Holles ending his notes the Royalist garrison in Bolingbroke Castle was besieged by Parliamentarian forces. The Royalists surrendered in the winter of 1643, and the entire castle was destroyed and was never rebuilt.

Bolsover Castle, Bolsover, Derbyshire

The 'Little Castle' you see today was begun in 1612 by Sir Charles Cavendish on the earthworks and ruins of a twelfth-century medieval castle built by the Peverel family. Sir Charles did not live to see it completed but the work was carried on by his sons, William and Charles. Willam Cavendish (1593–1676) was a flamboyant cavalier courtier and patron of the arts. Unusually for this period the accounts books for the castle also record female labour being involved in the construction of the castle. He chose no timid wallflower for his second wife when he married the prolific writer Margaret Lucas in 1645. Margaret's unusual fashions, manners, publications (some of which are seen as very early science fiction) and her 'unconventional interests' for the time drew some derision. The diarist Samuel Pepys would describe her as 'mad, conceited and ridiculous'; some would even call her 'Mad Madge'.

William was a staunch Royalist. He was created 1st Duke of Newcastle upon Tyne, was made a commander in the King's Army and even styled himself 'Prince William Cavendish' during the Civil War. Bolsover Castle remained in the Cavendish family and was one of the seats of the earls and dukes of Portland for many years. It was left unoccupied for long periods and by the 1880s had fallen into neglect.

The following account of a visit to Bolsover in its latter years of habitation was published in *The Spiritualist* on Friday 11 February 1881:

> The most delightful book published in England last year, be the second what it may, is Mr Louis Jennings's *Rambles among the Hills*, a worthy successor to his other charming book *Field Paths and Green Lanes*. Few men know more of the sequestered remote nooks of this fairyland of ours than he, and in his sixth chapter he declares that of all the houses he has seen, Bolsover Castle, in Derbyshire, is the most weird and ghostly – a place of mystery, where the spirit of the past still holds unbroken sway.
>
> To enter its strange portals is to step back suddenly into the shade of vanished centuries. Built by William de Peveril, the son of William the Conqueror, eight hundred years and more of strange eventful history have gathered round this grim and lonely castle. From the days of John, when it was stoutly defended against the Barons, to the time of the Commonwealth, when it was captured by Cromwell, sieges and battles have surged around its walls. It is now ruinous and mouldering, and when Mr Jennings visited it last year, and after passing through crumbling gateways, rapping without answer at many doors, and penetrating at last into a gallery, all unroofed and desolate with ten lofty windows, large and stately enough for a church, and still seeing no one, the mysterious influences of the place began to steal into his blood.
>
> At last after much knocking and hammering, an old woman came up panting from some region below, and guided him into an ancient hall, vaulted, with stone pillars, and mouldering portraits on the walls, of men and women

who lived and died three hundred years ago, and thence on through other ancient rooms, panelled and vaulted, and everything in them very old. One of them was called 'Mary Queen of Scots Prison', for in this weird house too was poor Mary a prisoner. 'There was an aspect,' writes Mr Jennings, 'about all these rooms which I have never seen elsewhere, and which I cannot describe. "It looks like a haunted house," said I to the woman. "You would say so if you lived here," she replied, but at that moment she said no more. She opened a little door, and remarked, "This bed-room is called Hell." Truly an uncommon name for a bed-room, but it was an uncommon room, with mutilated paintings on the ceiling and walls, and a spectral appearance all round. "Very strange noises are heard here at night," said the old woman, "but we do not mind them, they are heard all over the house."

As I passed back through they rooms they filled me with a feeling which I cannot explain. It may seem that I am drawing an over-coloured picture, or taking a page from Mrs. Radcliffe' s novels; but it is not, I truly describe what I saw, and how it impressed me, and I only know that from the moment the outer door was closed, an influence which I have never felt within any walls before came over me, and comes back perfectly clear and fresh to my recollection whenever I think of Bolsover Castle.

'We went downstairs,' Mr Jennings goes on to say, 'below the house itself to the cellars and passages which are said to be the remains of the Norman structure. There was a high vaulted the chamber now used as a kitchen and an ancient stone passage connected with of a sort of crypt, beneath which, as the old woman said, and I can neither verify nor disprove her account, but am content to take it as I received it – is a church never opened since the days of William de Peveril, son of the Conqueror.

'Our voices had a hollow sound, my footsteps awakened echoes from every corner. There must be some large empty space beneath the stone floor, but what it was used for in other days no one seemed to know. They say it has never been opened or examined. "This," I said in jest, "is where all your voices and ghosts come from." But the old women answered very seriously. "It is, sir, and when the family are here, the servants will not come down except by twos and threes. Oh, many people have seen things here besides me. Something bad has been done here, sir, and when they open that church below, they'll find it out. Just where you stand by that door, I have several times seen a lady and gentleman – only for a moment or two for they come like a flash. When I have been sitting in the kitchen, not thinking of any such thing, they stood there – the gentleman with ruffles on, the lady with a scarf round her waist. … I never believed in ghosts, but I have seen them. I am used to it now and don't mind it. But we do not like the noises. because they disturb us. Not long ago my husband, who comes here at night, and I, could not sleep at all, and we thought at last that somebody had got shut up in the castle, for some children had been here that day. So, we lit a candle, and went all over it, but there was nothing, only the voices following us, and keeping on worse than ever after we left the rooms, though they stopped while we were in them."

No wonder Mr Jennings felt the influences of this gruesome Castle, although evidently a smart wide-awake man, and, to judge from his looks, not at all tinctured with dreaminess, and quite a stranger to Spiritualism.

Now for a suggestion. Let a deputation or committee of Spiritualists, including a medium or two, and some clairvoyants, instead of pottering at dark seances in London drawing-rooms, and going through the old weary monotonous experiences of touches, strokings, tappings, tambourine-clatterings, gleams of floating faces, stupid parleys speed with stupid jokes, all leading to nothing, betake themselves to Bolsover Castle, explore the haunted rooms with their spiritual eyes and ears wide open, and hold vigils in the ghostly kitchen over the mysterious buried church. Let the clairvoyant eyes be intent and the medial perceptions all at full strain, and then let them return and recount their experiences, which ought to be worth hearing.[2]

Bolsover Castle was left uninhabited from 1883 until 1945 when it was given to the nation by the William Cavendish-Bentinck, 7th Duke of Portland (1893–1977). The buildings were stabilised by the Ministry of Works and today it is open to the public. The foliage that crept across those ancient walls has been cleared away but it still retains a great deal of atmosphere, especially inside the accessible rooms when it is quiet. This is not a castle with named spirits; it is haunted by many spirits who make themselves known by their presence and occasional sounds such as the cry of a baby or what feels like the touch of a child's hand.

One of the few ghosts that has been identified is William Cavendish, 1st Duke of Newcastle, who is believed to give his presence away with exotic smells when he is around and by touching the legs and faces of female visitors. The Hell Bedroom is still there but is now known as the Elysium Closet. The legend persists if the words 'sleep no more' are uttered within its walls during the hours of darkness, death will swiftly follow. I do not advise trying it, even in jest.

The ghostly activity continues to this day, doors slam and objects are found to have been mysteriously moved, night security guards have seen inexplicable lights, workmen have witnessed a woman 'disappear through a wall', and both staff and visitors have felt themselves being pushed by unseen hands. In one particularly disturbing incident a member of staff locked up the property for the night and as she walked away she heard a scream that got louder and louder. When she returned to the castle to investigate, she found nobody there. Bolsover Castle was voted the most haunted site by English Heritage staff in 2017.

Dudley Castle, Dudley, West Midlands

Dudley Castle began as wooden motte-and-bailey castle that was built on a huge outcrop of Wenlock limestone by Ansculf de Picquigny, a Norman who had fought at the Battle of Hastings in 1066. Rebuilt as a stone fortification during the twelfth century, this castle was subsequently demolished on the orders of Henry II. The third and final castle was begun by Roger de Somery in 1262 and was continued after his death in 1272 by his heirs.

During the English Civil War Dudley Castle was a Royalist garrison that was besieged by Parliamentary forces in 1644; it was finally surrendered to forces led by Sir William Brereton on 13 May 1646. Consequently, the castle was slighted (partially demolished) on the orders of Parliament the same year. Many of the residential buildings within the castle were also destroyed by a fire in 1750. In the nineteenth century the castle ruins were cleared up and made into a 'romantic ruin' for visitors to enjoy and events to be held – they now have Dudley Zoo in their grounds too.

Dudley Castle is believed to be one of the most haunted castles in the Midlands. In the 1970s newspapers reported such paranormal activity as cutlery being rearranged and the piano being played when there is nobody in the Queen Mary ballroom and disembodied voices being heard in the undercroft of the chapel.[3]

In fact, the chapel undercroft contains a stone coffin believed to have held the body of John Somery, last of the line, who died in 1321. He was one of the most feared lords of the castle and it really does not seem as if his spirit wants to leave. In is this area disembodied legs, thought to be those of John's ghost, have been seen, items of clothing have been pulled and bodies prodded by unseen hands. Disconcertingly, grinding and scraping noises of stone on stone, as if a stone coffin lid is being slid to the side have also been heard.

The ruins are also haunted by the 'Grey Lady', believed to be the ghost of Dorothy Beaumont whose baby daughter died shortly after she gave birth and Dorothy died soon afterwards of complications. Her dying wish was that she should be buried next to her baby and that her husband should attend their funeral. Neither of these happened and her ghost wanders the castle looking perturbed and lost, perhaps still seeking her baby. The ghost of a lone English Civil War drummer boy who was killed by a musket ball is said to haunt the castle too. If you hear the beat and roll of his drum it is said to presage bad luck.

In 1978 a group from Wolverhampton Polytechnic students' union caving club explored caves under the castle that had not been used since the Second World War. No previous reports had been made of the area being haunted but one of the students, John Merris, happened to take a photograph that showed half a transparent figure with its arms crossed.[4]

In the 1990s another spate of ghost sightings were witnessed from outside the castle at night when shadowy figures were seen moving around the battlements after the castle was shut for the day.[5]

Fillingham Castle, Fillingham, Lincolnshire

Fillingham Castle is a private home, a castellated neo-Gothic stone mansion built by Sir Cecil Wray in 1760. The grounds are haunted by a tall man who rides a large white horse at a gallop through the park. The spectre known as the 'Green Lady' has also been spotted in the grounds around the castle. Local legend states that she is the spirit of a suicide who was jilted by her lover. With no other candidates springing out from the history of the castle, I wonder if the spirit of Alexandrina Douglas who died suddenly at the castle could still linger there? The *Lincolnshire Echo* of 7 October 1897 reported:

> Dr Mitchinson, District Coroner, held an inquest at Fillingham Castle yesterday, on the body of Alexandrina Douglas, housekeeper to Mr and Mrs Portman-Dalton. The deceased, who was 29 years of age, and came from Scotland, had died very suddenly the previous morning. It appeared that for some time she had been in ill-health and had complained of headache and shortness of breath. About ten months ago, Dr Boulton, of Ingham, saw her for indigestion, and recently Mrs Portman-Dalton consulted her medical man in London about her, who warned her that there was defective circulation.
>
> On Tuesday morning she was called as usual, by the scullery maid, at a quarter past seven and seemed as usual. Half an hour later she gave the customary orders to the kitchen maid, who went into her room, and who at five minutes past eight took her a post letter and found her lying across the bed partly dressed. She said she had fainted, and after drinking a cup of water said she felt, better. The kitchen maid then fetched her a cup of tea, and she drank a little. Miss Roberry, ladies' maid, went to see her, and after a time left her, telling her if she did not feel well to come across to her room. Ten minutes afterwards Miss Roberry went back to the room and found her lying on the bed gasping, and evidently in great pain. Some brandy was fetched, and she swallowed a little, hot flannels being also applied, but she expired before the arrival of Dr Boulton, who had been sent for.

> Dr Boulton stated that on his arrival at about a quarter past ten he found that life had evidently been extinct for about an hour. There were no marks of injury, than natural causes. He was of opinion that death had resulted from failure of the heart's action. A juryman stated that he met the deceased returning from a walk, when she looked tired and apparently short of breath. The jury at once returned a verdict in accordance with the medical evidence.[6]

Clearly Miss Douglas had unfinished business heading the staff at the castle; one can only wonder if she had left Scotland having been jilted in love, wore a green dress and literally died of a broken heart.

Goodrich Castle, Goodrich, Herefordshire

Goodrich Castle is believed to have been built by Godric of Mappestone as an earth-and-wood fortification shortly after the Norman Conquest to command a key location between Monmouth and Ross-on-Wye. In the middle of the twelfth century the original castle was replaced with a stone keep,

In 1247 the castle passed by marriage to William de Valence, half-brother of Henry III. Valence's marriage to Joan de Munchensi not only brought him the castle, but it also made him rich with her family money and gave him the title of Earl of Pembroke. He then set about redeveloping and expanding the castle into a concentric structure that combined commodious living quarters with extensive defences.

Goodrich Castle exchanged hands to be occupied by both Parliament and Royalist forces during the English Civil War. The final siege was by Parliamentary Colonel John Birch in 1646. The Royalists who had garrisoned the castle surrendered to Birch, whose attacks on the castle had been ably assisted by a huge mortar named 'Roaring Meg'. The following year Parliament ordered that the castle should be slighted so it could never be defended again and it began a descent into ruin. By the end of the eighteenth century, however, Goodrich Castle had become a picturesque ruin and a popular subject for painters and poets; its praises were sung by William Wordsworth as the 'noblest ruin in Herefordshire'.

The haunting of Goodrich Castle is said to date from those dark years of the English Civil War. A young Royalist officer and his lover, named in some accounts as simply Alice and Clifford, tragically drowned in the River Wye along with their horses while attempting to escape from the besieged castle in 1646. Their ghosts are mounted on horseback, he at the reins and she riding pillion; they are seen struggling in the river whenever a heavy storm hits or the river is in spate. The couple has also been spotted standing in the ruins of the castle, probably on the spot where they made their final decision to risk their lives and make their break for freedom.

Hopton Castle, Hopton, Shropshire

During the Civil War Hopton Castle was one of the few fortresses to be held for the Parliament in the west of England. In 1644 Royalist commander Sir Michael Woodhouse laid siege to the castle with a force of about 500 men. The castle was garrisoned by about 30 Roundheads under the command of Colonel Samuel More. The castle had withstood two previous attacks. I have to admit in the face of superior numbers I admire More who refused to acknowledge the first message offering terms of surrender because it was delivered 'without drum or trumpet'. After the second attack the terms of surrender were offered with the appropriate musical accompaniment but were still turned down.

Woodhouse left, regrouped and returned with a heavier armoury including three massive siege guns. More held out for two weeks but was eventually left with no other option than to surrender. The best terms he could hope for were that the lives of his men would be spared. They surrendered on the understanding their fate would be decided by Woodhouse.

More was given safe conduct and removed to a house in the village, but Woodhouse decided to give the remaining men of the garrison no quarter. A Parliamentary account records these men as having their hands cut off, then being stoned or drowned in a ditch. According to another account, not only were all the men killed, but the old steward of the castle was offered the gentler option of being able to rest his old legs and sit in a chair, and then have his throat cut. The 'Hopton Quarter' soon became a byword for treacherous treatment. The ghosts of the Roundheads return to haunt the castle each year on 14 March, the anniversary of their massacre.

Kenilworth Castle, Kenilworth, Warwickshire

In its Elizabethan heyday Kenilworth Castle was one of one of the great royal castles of England. First built in the 1120s, it was expanded by King John. Under John of Gaunt the castle was repaired and, from 1391 onwards, was converted from a feudal stronghold into a palace. Queen Elizabeth I granted Kenilworth Castle to her favourite, Robert Dudley, in 1563 and created him Earl of Leicester the following year. Dudley would invest a fortune redeveloping the old castle and its grounds into a palace and gardens fit for his queen. Although it is in ruins today, they still give a good idea of just how impressive this Elizabethan palace was. That said, the ghosts of Kenilworth are, in the main, not the royals and nobles who were there over the centuries.

The castle stables have the ghost of a young boy who occasionally appears there along with ghostly horses and even chickens. The castle gatehouse is claimed to be haunted by several ghosts including a little girl who asks for her father, an old woman who appears to break a candle repeatedly and an antique wooden cot in an Elizabethan bedroom that is rocked by an unseen hand. Cold spots and invisible presences have also been felt across the site by visitors and staff, but no stories seem to have survived that offer any explanation for these hauntings. Only the shadowy figure of a man dressed in black is said to be the spirit of a gentleman who was killed in a duel.

A feature in the *Coventry Herald* in February 1915 adds something new to the hauntings, telling of a spectral carriage and the baronet who left with some unexpected souvenirs after his visit to Kenilworth Castle:

> A phantom carriage, with phantom horses, phantom coachman, and a phantom lady inside is said to issue forth from Kenilworth Castle ruins once in the year, says Canon Caswell in the current issue of the St Austin's (Kenilworth) Parish Magazine.
>
> At the midnight hour, it noisily makes for Gibbet Hill, and thence in a bee-line it rushes pell-mell over hedges and

ditches to Gosford Green. I have never met anyone who has seen the start, but I know some one who listens for its approach to the Green – and hears it! Kenilworth Castle never gives me the idea of its being haunted as Cryficld, or Redfen, or Stoneleigh does. But read the next paragraph seriously.

On my table lies a pamphlet of 25 pages, entitled 'A Lecture on Spiritism' presently sent me, presumably by the lecturer himself – a baronet of the United Kingdom … The passage I quote and will be interesting to visitors and residents alike:

'On one occasion I spent some hours in the ruins of Kenilworth Castle with some friends who lived near there. It was in the very early days of my study of spiritism, and I never had any thoughts of my visit being connected with spirit manifestations; but when I attended a seance some weeks or so after, several – four or five – materialised forms came to me one after another, all dressed in Elizabethan costume, with ruffle and full sleeves complete. … For the moment I had quite forgotten about my visit, and I asked the 'controls' for an explanation as who the visitors were. They replied that they had followed from some place I had recently visited connected with their period, and I then remembered Kenilworth. Two were female forms and one of the male entities they said was Sir Walter Raliegh.'[7]

Lincoln Castle, Lincoln, Lincolnshire

Lincoln Castle, in fact, the whole historic city centre of Lincoln, is a great place to visit if you love historical buildings, history and atmosphere. The castle was built in the eleventh century on the site of an earlier Roman fortress. It contains a courthouse – that still operates as a crown court to this day – and prison. The towers around the curtain wall include the Cobb Tower where wooden gallows were assembled upon its roof and thirty-eight condemned prisoners were publicly executed there between 1817 and 1859. The bodies of the executed were then buried within the walls of the castle in the grounds of the Lucy Tower. These graves, marked with low headstones bearing the initials of the felons and the date of their execution, are still in situ.

The red-brick Georgian gaol was built in 1788, and in 1848 the old felons' wing was demolished and a new prison wing built to Victorian standards was erected. This was used to hold male, female and child prisoners for short terms as they awaited trial as well as convicts pending removal elsewhere to serve their sentences. The prison was run on the separate and silent system; the inmates wore convict uniforms and masks that blinkered their eyes so they would constantly look downwards and prevented felons from recognising each other. If any prisoner was caught speaking to another he would be punished.

The prison chapel is one of only two surviving examples of a separate system chapel designed and built so that each prisoner could only see the chaplain, and not each other. It certainly has atmosphere. Staff have observed strange lights inside the chapel when it was locked and should have been empty and doors have been reported to open and close by themselves. Strong presences and sensations are felt in the compartments of the chapel. In fact, the whole historic site can leave visitors with the unnerving feeling they are being watched.

A horse and a rider are also said to haunt the area, the sound of hoofbeats heard near the castle gates. According to a local legend, the ghostly rider was close friend of a local lord who had been wrongly sentenced to death. The rider had been tasked with delivering a pardon from the king to save his friend, but unfortunately, he did not arrive in time to stop the execution.

The paranormal activity seems to centre on the prison and towers associated with executions and burials of those hanged. One of the most frequently sighted ghosts is a lady carrying a baby seen walking down the stairs of the Victorian Women's Prison. Sounds of day-to-day life in the prison, the jangling of keys, footsteps in studded boots, disembodied voices, moans, groans and even screams have been known to play out within the walls.

Poacher William Clarke (alias Slenderman) was hanged on 26 March 1877 for the murder of gamekeeper Henry Walker. Clarke was last person to be executed at Lincoln Castle and his ghost along with his faithful lurcher are said to haunt the grounds of the castle and the nearby Strugglers Inn where Clarke often used to drink. The dog was taken in by the landlord of the Strugglers after Clarke's execution, but it soon pined away for his master. The dog was stuffed and put on show in the pub for many years and is now on display at Lincoln Castle.

The ghost of Mary Ann Milner (27) is said to haunt the cell in the prison where she committed suicide by hanging herself with the silk scarf she had worn at her trial just hours before she was due to be publicly executed on 30 July 1847. Milner had been indicted on three separate accounts of wilful murder by the administration of arsenic to three women, Mary Milner her mother-in-law, Hannah Jickels her sister-in-law and Ellen Jickels her niece. Her father-in-law was also poisoned by her hand but had recovered only to be 'reduced to imbecility from the effects of poison'. The only apparent motive for her crime, committed at Barnetby-le-Wold near Brigg, was to obtain payouts from a burial society. Cleared on the first count of murder, Milner was faced by conclusive evidence that Hannah Jickels had died from eating a pancake containing arsenic that she had given to her. After a deliberation of twenty minutes the jury returned a verdict of 'guilty'. The third indictment for the murder of her niece was not proceeded with. Milner never evinced the slightest emotion nor shed a single tear throughout her trial. The large crowd that had gathered below the Cobb Tower had to leave disappointed after being denied the theatre of her execution.

The most famous ghost sighting at Lincoln Castle is that of a woman dressed in black in and around the prison near where the execution shed used to stand. It has been suggested this is the ghost of Priscilla Biggadike (29) who went to her death wearing a black mourning dress on 28 December 1868. Her story is worth telling because it remains one of the most notorious in the annals of Lincolnshire criminal history. Priscilla and her husband Richard Biggadike (30), a well sinker, lived in the rural village of Mareham-le-Fen, about 6 miles from Horncastle. They shared their house, although there was just one room for sleeping, with their three children and two male lodgers named George Ironmonger and rat catcher Thomas Proctor. Mr Biggadike was in the habit of leaving his wife in bed when he went to work but he had become concerned that Proctor and Priscilla were having an affair and even began to wonder if their last child was a product of the clandestine relationship.

On 30 September Richard sat down to a meal of mutton followed by shortcake made by Priscilla. Within ten minutes he was retching and stuck down with excruciating pain in his stomach, He died in agony the following morning. Analysis of his stomach contents by Professor

Taylor revealed a large quantity of arsenic. When suspicion fell upon Priscilla, who had made comments to the effect she wished her husband dead, she immediately tried to deflect them onto Proctor whom she said she had seen put a white powder into a teacup and also into the medicine ordered for her husband, and he was taken into custody.

The confused statements made by Pricilla aroused suspicion and she was also arrested. Proctor and Biggadike would stand trial before the Assizes. The case against Proctor did not hold up and he was soon acquitted and the main thrust of the prosecution was turned upon Priscilla. She was found guilty of the murder on what was essentially circumstantial evidence and sentenced to death. Despite the prison chaplain imploring her to confess as she stood on the gallows. Priscilla firmly denied she had administered the poison that killed her husband.

Rather than being hanged in public atop the Cobb Tower Priscilla was hanged in private in a shed that housed the gallows. As she was prepared by executioner Thomas Askern, her last words before the traps fell were 'Oh! You won't hang me!' Once she had dropped it was noted 'she appeared to suffer a good deal before her strong vital powers succumbed'. The twist in this tale came in 1882 as Thomas Proctor was lying on his death bed and confessed it was he who had administered the poison that killed Richard Biggadike.

Ludlow Castle, Ludlow, Shropshire

Walter de Lacy was granted the manor of Stanton, which contained the site of what has become present-day Ludlow, and founded the castle around 1075; after his death in 1085 the construction of the stone fortifications was carried on by his sons. The castle remained in the hands of the de Lacy family until the end of the early fourteenth century when it passed by marriage to the Mortimer family who are responsible for much of the redevelopment and construction of the castle we see today.

Ludlow Castle certainly played its part in history and has been host and home to kings and princes over the centuries. Edward IV (1442–83) visited the castle regularly and established a council there to govern his estates in Wales. Prince Edward (later to become one of the 'Princes in the Tower') was in residence at Ludlow when he learned of the death of his father, and assumed the title of King Edward V.

Mary Tudor spent nineteen months at Ludlow overseeing the Council of the Marches between 1525 and 1528 and the future Charles I was declared Prince of Wales in the castle by James I at Ludlow Castle in 1616. When the English Civil War broke out, Ludlow came out on the side of the Royalists and a garrison was placed there under Sir Michael Woodhouse.

Sir William Brereton and Colonel John Birch led a Parliamentary army from Hereford to take Ludlow in April 1646. After a short siege, Woodhouse surrendered the castle and town and received good terms on 26 May (which is a lot more than those who surrendered to Woodhouse at Hopton Castle had received). Ludlow Castle was abandoned after 1689 and local people used some of the castle materials as a ready supply of building materials. Fortunately, it was saved in time and much of the castle still stands intact or has been sympathetically restored.

The haunting of the castle is said to date to 1139 when Ludlow Castle was holding out against King Stephen. A lady of the castle retinue named Marion de la Bruyère had fallen in love with a knight, Arnold de Lys, but alas he was on the side of Stephen. Determined that nothing should keep them apart Marion would lower a rope over the castle wall so her lover could join her. One night, however, he did not come alone; he did not take the rope up after him as usual, but he left it dangling so his compatriots could follow him, and so they did and the castle was thus taken.

Marion was heartbroken by her lover's betrayal and she withdrew his dagger from his belt and stabbed him through the heart. She then climbed the high Pendover Tower and threw herself over the battlements onto rocks below. Her ghost, known as the 'White Woman', has occasionally been seen around the castle and even repeating her terrible end as the evening dusk gathers. It is said that on the anniversary of her suicide her screams can be heard as she plummets down, but no sickening thud is heard as he hits the ground – she just disappears.

Another story tells of a family who were evacuated from Liverpool to Ludlow during the Second World War who spent four months in part of the castle. While there they heard rappings, bangs and doors opening and closing when no one was about. There are also numerous accounts from staff and visitors over the years of the strange and eerie sounds of heavy breathing or gasping for breath heard distinctly around battlements and which even seem to resonate from the walls of The Hanging Tower.

Moreton Corbet Castle, Moreton Corbet, Shropshire

Moreton Corbet Castle is a wonderfully picturesque location where there are considerable ruins of both a medieval castle keep and an Elizabethan manor house. During the English Civil War, Moreton Castle was used as part of Royalist defences of Shrewsbury and the castle withstood siege on several occasions. It was captured by a small Parliamentarian force during a night attack in September 1644.

The castle was repaired after the war but by the late seventeenth century it had been abandoned. The story of the haunting of this place dates to the reign of King James I (1566–1625) when the Corbet family who lived in the house at the time gave shelter to a Puritan named Paul Holmyard. As Holmyard made himself at home he expressed increasingly fanatical views, and it all got too much for the Corbets and they asked Holmyard to leave. Holmyard went to live for some time in the local woods, where he just seethed with anger. He returned to the castle once more to issue a curse:

> *Woe unto thee, hard hearted man, the lord has hardened thy heart as he hardened the heart of the Pharaoh, to thine own destruction.*
>
> *Rejoice not in thy riches, not in monuments of thy pride, for neither thou, nor thy children, nor thy children's children shall inhabit these halls.*
>
> *They shall be given up to desolation; snakes, vipers and unclean beasts shall make it their refuge, and thy home shall be full of doleful creatures.*

Despite the building of the castle not yet being complete, the Corbet family were said to have been so terrified of the curse that they fled the house never to return and it fell into ruin. Local legend tells of the bedraggled ghostly figure of Holmyard patrolling the ruins on a moonlit night to ensure they stay that way.

Nottingham Castle, Nottingham, Nottinghamshire

Nottingham Castle, steeped in the folkloric tales of Robin Hood. looms above the town of Nottingham high on a hill. The original castle was built shortly after the Norman Conquest, but it was subsequently razed to the ground and rebuilt several times. Its walls and tunnels beneath however still retain their ghosts, notably Queen Isabella and her lover Roger Mortimer who brought about the cruel demise of her husband King Edward II at Berkeley Castle, whose voice and footsteps are believed to have been heard in the subterranean passages.

In the 1920s a number of mysterious noises were reported to be heard emanating from the underground passages of the castle, especially Mortimer's Hole and in the cellars of properties that adjoined the subterranean passages on Standard Hill. Several vigils were held during the national spiritualists' conference at Nottingham in March 1921 and were reported in national and local newspapers:

> One of a watching party in a house communicating with the castle's underground dungeons, a Mr D. Roberts, of Liverpool, in an interview with a 'Daily News' representative declared that the clanking of the chains had been heard. … There are two stone beds in one of the dungeons to which prisoners were manacled and on one of these a pillow was placed before the dungeon was secured for the night. In the morning it had been moved to the other bed. Parties of investigators have had unpleasant experiences, it is said, owing to the advance and retreat of footsteps, which caused several visitors to fly in fright.[8]

A well-publicised seance was also held with London medium Miss Leslie presiding at the castle. Those present were Councillor Seely Whitby (Lord Mayor of Nottingham in 1922–23), local man and acclaimed portrait painter Mr Noel Denholm Davis, Mr P. T. Selbit (born Percy Thomas Tibbles), the magician who would be credited as the first to perform the illusion of 'sawing a woman in half', Mr Tom Jones ARCA, Mrs Butterworth, Mr S. W. Barlow-Vines, the editor of the *Evening News*, a reporter from the *Nottingham Journal* and local professional photographer Mr Walter Baker, who had his studio on Derby Road.

The group descended into Mortimer's Hole as the clock struck noon and once all were seated Miss Leslie asked for the candles that had been lit by their guide to be extinguished. She then asked the group to sing an old-fashioned song and the melody was soon reverberating around the room.

As they did so a 'filmy and phosphorescent figure of a man with a pointed chin' was beginning to form when Mr Seely Whitby, who was running late, recalled his arrival:

> The guide accompanied me down the steps of Mortimer's Hole. I heard what seemed to be a hymn floating up from the abysmal gloom below. I thought that it was a church service and struck a match. I then saw a circle of men and two ladies joining hands and chanting a dirge. Someone challenged me and suggested that I had faked the apparition. I stoutly deny this, and the guide will bear me out. I passed nothing and saw no one on the way down.

During the seance a number of those present told reporters that they believed they had seen three distinct figures which they felt were Mortimer, Queen Isabella and Edward III. Mr Selbit the illusionist admitted that he had posted a guide on the staircase to prevent any unauthorised exits or entrances. Had admitted that had been puzzled by the apparitions, concluding, 'It is a mystery, but I think I shall solve it.'[9]

With the town abuzz with these events the *Nottingham Journal* published a 300-year-old recipe of 'a celebrated alchemist', which was supposed to enable the person who created it 'to behold without difficulty or danger the most potent spirit of fayrie you may encounter'. I include it purely for interest, I do not advise trying it:

> A pint of Sallet-oyle, and put it in a vial glass but first wash it with rose water and mary-gold water; the flowers to be gathered towards the east. Wash it until the oyle become white, then put it in the glasse and then the buds of hollyhocks, the flowers of mary-gold, the flowers of toppes of wild thime, the bude of young hazle, and the thime must be gathered near the side of a hill where the fayries use to

> be, and take the grasse of a fayrie throne, then all those put into the oyle into the glasse, and sette it to dissolve three dayes in the sunne and then keep it for thy use.[10]

Queen Isabella has also been heard shouting from the battlements of Nottingham Castle. In one notable incident during the Second World War, a group of American GIs were walking past the castle one night and heard what they described as a woman screaming 'foreign words' from the battlements. When they told local people who knew the stories, they were told they must have heard the queen cry, '*Bel Fitz, Bel Fitz, ayez pitie du gentile Mortimer*', the words she is said to had cried when Edward III, Montacute, three Bohuns, and others stormed into Isabella's apartment in Nottingham Castle, and seized Mortimer.

Stokesay Castle, Stokesay, Shropshire

To be frank, Stokesay Castle is a gem. Regarded as the finest fortified manor house in England, it looks what it is, a wonderful thirteenth-century castle with a timber-framed great hall and solar built on top. It must be seen to be believed. Stokesay was originally owned by the de Lacy family, who built the first Ludlow Castle. Wealthy wool merchant Laurence de Ludlow bought the tenancy of the castle and received licence to crenellate from the king in 1291.

The lovely ocre gatehouse was built by Lord William Craven in 1640–41 is also superbly decorated with carvings of Adam and Eve, mythical creatures and dragons. Stokesay Castle was a Royalist garrison during the Civil War, but it surrendered with little bloodshed; even though the castle was ordered to be slighted most of the castle buildings were left undamaged.

The ghosts claimed to have been seen at Stokesay are an eighteenth-century highwayman and the ghost of an elderly woman smoking a clay pipe. There is even believed to be a poltergeist, who throws stock from the shelves in the shop. Most mysterious of all is the ghost of the 'Grey Lady', a woman wearing a long cloak whose features are hardly discernible beneath the hood she wears. It has been claimed that she has been seen gliding silently across the great hall.

People are said to have felt a chilling presence on the castle stairs that is believed to be the 'Grey Lady', and staff and visitors often speak of an uncomfortable feeling of being watched by unseen eyes around the castle. It is claimed the ghost of the 'Grey Lady' warns people off a casket of treasure hidden long ago somewhere in the castle. Believed to be a real hidden treasure, the *Weekly Despatch* newspaper in September 1902 mentioned the hidden chest at Stokesay Castle 'containing plate and jewels worth £50,000' (nearly £8 million in today's money) that was 'said to be actually in the vaults'.[11] For those who attempt to seek it and get a little too close, the spectral woman is said to whisper in their ear, 'Keep away from what is buried.' No one is known to have pushed on to find out what might happen if they disobeyed her warning.

Tamworth Castle, Tamworth, Staffordshire

Tamworth Castle had been the site of a fortification since ancient history when Robert Despenser built a motte-and-bailey castle there. Robert died without issue, so it passed to his niece who married Robert de Marmion. The Marmion family were hereditary champions of the dukes of Normandy and performed the same role for the new kings of England. They would hold Tamworth Castle for six generations from around 1100 until 1294.

King Alfred's granddaughter, Editha, had founded a convent at nearby Polesworth in the seventh century and their order existed quietly there until they were ejected by Robert de Marmion. The nuns prayed Editha would assist them from beyond the grave, and she appeared before Marmion after a banquet. St Editha's ghost warned him that unless the nuns were restored to their convent, he would meet an untimely death. She then struck Marmion on the side of his head with her crosier.

Marmion's agonised cries awoke the whole castle and the wound he suffered bled incessantly. The blood only stopped flowing and the pain ceased when he made his solemn promise that the nuns would be restored to Polesworth. The ghost of a 'Blackrobed Lady' is believed to be Editha who haunts the ancient staircase in Tamworth Castle that leads from the royal bedchamber to the tower.[12] It is also here that groans and moans of someone in a lot of pain have been heard and even recorded on tape on a number of occasions since the 1970s.

A ghost of a 'white lady', who appears 'arrayed in glistening robes, which shimmer in the moonlight', is also claimed to promenade along the terrace and has been seen on Lady's Meadow. She is also said to be a ghost of quite some antiquity who, according to local legend, has walked since she saw her lover killed by Sir Launcelot below the castle walls. Unable to live without her love, she committed suicide by throwing herself over the battlements of the castle.

In the early twentieth century it was believed both ghosts regularly appeared at Christmastime.[13]

Tutbury Castle, Tutbury, Staffordshire

Tutbury Castle began as a Norman castle built in 1071 and became the seat of the powerful Norman baron, Henry de Ferrers. The remains of the castle seen today date back to the later castle constructed in the fourteenth and fifteenth centuries. A Royalist stronghold during the English Civil War, it fell to Parliamentary forces after a siege and was destroyed, reducing it to ruins.

Elizabeth I believed Mary, Queen of Scots and her supporters to be a credible threat to the English throne, so she had Mary arrested and placed in the custody of George Talbot, 6th Earl of Shrewsbury who held her in his castles, away from the Scottish borders. Mary lodged as a prisoner at Tutbury Castle for the first time in 1569. She was provided with rooms that were furnished and was allowed her retinue. The Earl of Shrewsbury wrote of how Mary sat with his wife Bess of Hardwick, Countess of Shrewsbury in the countess's chamber at Tutbury with Lady Livingston and Mary Seton working at embroidery. It all sounds very homely, but Mary complained of Tutbury being more a hunting lodge than a castle, being draughty with damp plaster walls and having ill-fitting carpetry.

Leaving for Wingfield Manor after about two months at Tutbury Castle, Mary would be returned there again in 1585. This time the queen's bedchamber would be located on the top floor of her lodgings; it would have wall hangings and a tent of tapestries over her bed to keep out draughts and keep the warmth in. She had her retinue, her own guards (although they were disarmed of their pistols) and was even provided with a billiard table, but she hated the place.

Mary, Queen of Scots left Tutbury Castle in December 1585 never to return while she was alive, but her ghost has been seen in the castle and around the grounds on numerous occasions by staff and visitors. She is said to appear as solid as in life; in one reported incident in 2004 she appeared standing at the top of the South Tower, peering down and was seen by a group of forty visitors.

Among the other spirits claimed to have been seen at the castle are a little boy and a young girl, and a ghost known as 'The Keeper' is said to appear in full armour at John of Gaunt's Gateway. The paranormal activity, strange misty and shadowy figures that have been seen in the king's bedroom in the castle over the years have led some to believe it to be one of the most haunted rooms in the country.

Warwick Castle, Warwick, Warwickshire

Over the years it seems the number of ghosts at Warwick Castle has increased and some of their stories have changed in the retelling, as many stories do. I am inclined towards the earlier versions of the stories. Francis Greville, 5th Earl of Warwick and Brooke discusses the ghosts in his family seat in his autobiography *Memories of Sixty Years* (1917) and offers a very fair assessment of what does and does not haunt Warwick Castle. The earl freely confessed he had never seen or heard a ghost himself, but he seems to have kept an open mind. He mentions that his mother 'used to hear uncanny noises'. He recalled Archdeacon Colley 'came to the castle several times and held seances in the oak bedroom … he brought a medium from Birmingham, and I believed they raised or saw a little girl carrying flowers', adding, 'I have often thought how interesting it would be to invite Sir Oliver Lodge over, or other sympathiser of equal eminence, if such there be, and ask him if he could establish communication with some of the great figures that have stayed in the castle.' The earl explained:

> The castle, though the town of Warwick lies by its side, is very quiet a night. No sounds were audible until, in the past few years, express trains passed it in the distance over the Great Western and North Western lines. Every sound seems to have something akin to the quality of surprise, and

> undoubtedly some that are due to perfectly natural causes have been misinterpreted. I remember the mysterious rapping in Guy's Tower that was attributed to ghosts, until somebody had a brain-wave and discovered that it was due to the rapping of the halyard cord against the flagstaff!'[14]

Of the known hauntings within the historic walls, he recounted:

> They say that at midnight a lady rides through the State Rooms on a white horse; while in the courtyard may be seen the ghost of the Dun Cow that Guy, Earl of Warwick, killed on Dunsmore Heath ... I have been unable to learn why the ghost of the cow should still parade the courtyard. There is said to be another apparition of an old woman who walks along the corridors by day. My wife had seen her twice. She moves slowly and with averted face, silent and intangible. She is gone almost as soon as seen.[15]

A year later the Reverend James Harvey Bloom, who would go on to write *Folk Lore, Old Customs, and Superstitions in Shakespeare Land* (1929), wrote of a ghost at Warwick Castle in *Notes and Queries* (1918):

> An ancient dame [named in some accounts as Moll Bloxham] had the privilege of selling spare milk, and, by a system not unknown to modern milk vendors, she so cheated her customers that the Earl, hearing of it, cancelled the privilege. She then bewitched the Castle usually in the form of a black dog. The chaplain, with the Vicars of St Mary's and St Nicholas's, brought the evil one to rest by reading passages of Scripture, and eventually followed the witch in the form of a dog to the height of Caesar's Tower, from which she or it sprang into the stream, to a chamber prepared under the mill dam.[16]

Another article, published in the *Nottingham Evening Post* in October 1926, tells of how the ghost of Sir Guy of Warwick, the brave knight who slayed the Dun Cow, haunts Warwick Castle:

> Guy is supposed to walk from one end of the inhabited part of the castle to the other, that is to say, he traverses a distance of about a quarter of a mile, starting at Caesar's Tower and finishing at the Water Tower. A former Bailiff to the present Lord Warwick's grandfather always told a vivid tale of how, when he was waiting on the route of the ghost's peregrinations, he heard colossal footsteps approach, pass him, and then go on, when he could actually see nothing. … Francess, Countess of Warwick, the mother of the present Earl, also relates that when she was first married and was sleeping in a lonely section of the house on the direct route, she heard the same footsteps, which were enormously magnified, and as at that time all the carpets had been removed, the steps echoed from end to end of the building. The dogs in her rooms became panic-stricken and cowered under the bed.

For those who are not familiar with the story of the Dun Cow, in brief it is a legendary tale of a huge dun cow, said to be 12 feet high and 18 feet long that emerged from a forest in Warwickshire and laid waste to the land, devouring livestock and people, terrifying all who saw the cow to run for their lives.

The man the local people thought could save them was Guy of Warwick but alas he had recently left to fight in France. The king's messengers carried the appeals for some brave knight to come to the aid of the people of Warwickshire for fine reward. They soon came to reach Guy of Warwick whose departure had been delayed as the ship that was going to take him and the other knights across to France was waiting for a severe storm at sea to subside before leaving port. Brave Guy of Warwick immediately mounted his horse and set off to return to his home county. As he crossed the border he began to see the bones of the animals, the wrecked villages and deserted cottages that had been left in the wake of the Dun Cow. Following the trail of wreckage and the sound of its bellow, Guy tracked the cow down. Tethering his horse a safe distance away, Guy fought the cow on foot. After a dramatic fight he slew the monster cow, peace was restored to the land and Guy was given the rich reward by the king. A rib of the infamous Dun Cow was preserved and has been displayed at Warwick Castle ever since.

The article concludes with the most probable ghost of all at Warwick Castle:

> The 'Grey Lady,' however, whose origin is wrapped in mystery, has been seen by many members of the family up to the present day. The grandmother of the present Earl was always seeing her, while many servants have borne witness to catching a glimpse of her furtive figure flitting about the long corridors. Doors open without reason, the 'Grey Lady' appears and then passes on, and when the astonished spectator goes to find her there is nothing.[17]

Above: Bolsover Castle, Derbyshire, c. 1905. The 'Little Castle' is haunted by several ghosts, including William Cavendish, 1st Duke of Newcastle who died in 1676, and whose icy touch is occasionally felt by female visitors.

Below: The gateway of Carlisle Castle, Cumbria, c. 1910. Haunted by several soldierly spectres, is the shadowy figure behind the soldier on the right the ghost of a dead comrade?

Above: The impressive gatehouse of Lancaster Castle, Lancashire, c. 1900. Mother Demdike, one of the accused 'Pendle Witches', haunts the castle dungeon where she died in 1612.

Below: One of the haunted corridors of Naworth Castle, Cumbria, c. 1900, where the ghost of the betrayed 'Woman in White' is said to walk.

Barnard Castle, County Durham, c. 1910, said to be haunted by 'Lady Ann Day' and the notorious demonic lantern man 'Briggy Dobbie'.

Above: Blenkinsopp Castle, Northumberland, c. 1900, haunted by the mysterious 'White Lady', said to be the guardian of a hidden treasure.

Below: Chillingham Castle, Northumberland, 2022, has a long and well-documented history of its ghosts and is described as 'Britain's Most Haunted Castle'.

Above: Chipchase Castle, Northumberland, c. 1910. The castle was so haunted in the 1930s they had had problems retaining servants.

Below: Featherstone Castle, Northumberland, c. 1900. The hall of the castle and the wooded pass at Pynkinscleugh is ridden through by a ghostly wedding party on horseback on the anniversary of their slaughter.

Raby Castle, Northumberland, c. 1890. The ghost of the formidable Lady Elizabeth Vane (1657–1725), 'The Old Hell Cat', is said to haunt the roof, angrily pacing back and forth as she knits with red hot needles.

Above: The gatehouse entrance to Lincoln Castle Prison, c. 1900. The ghosts of some of those executed for murder and those who died while in the prison are said to haunt it.

Below: Ludlow Castle, Shropshire, c. 1900. These ruins are haunted by Marion de la Bruyère who was betrayed by her lover, so she stabbed him then threw herself over the battlements.

Above: Stokesay Castle, Shropshire c. 1910, a thirteenth-century castle with a timber-framed great hall and solar built on top. It is haunted by several ghosts including a highwayman and the 'Grey Lady'.

Below: The tomb of Katherine Parr (1512–48), sixth and final wife of Henry VIII in the chapel at Sudeley Castle, Gloucestershire. Woe betide anyone who disturbed the bones of the dead queen.

The haunted stairway at Castle Rising, Norfolk, 2007. Said to be haunted by Queen Isabella, 'the She-Wolf of France', the walls exude a powerful sense of history here.

Above: Norwich Castle, Norfolk, 2015. The mound and galleries within are haunted by the ghosts of three women who were publicly executed on the gallows on the bridge over the castle ditches.

Below: The White Tower, the most famous keep in the world, 2023. The Tower of London is one of the most infamously haunted places in Britain.

Above: Arundel Castle, Sussex, c. 1900, is haunted by a cavalier in a blue silk doublet in the library, a boy who was worked to death in the kitchen and even the ghostly rumble of Cromwell's cannon has been heard.

Below: Chilham Castle, Kent, c. 1920. Actor Kim Novak encountered the ghost of the 'White Lady' on the stairs while filming here in 1965.

Dover Castle, Kent, c. 1935. Known as 'the Key to England', it is haunted by the ghost of a headless drummer boy from the time of the Napoleonic wars.

Above: Hastings Castle, Sussex, c. 1910 haunted by a 'woman in white' said to be the ghost of a nun. It is believed this spectre was contacted at a seance in the castle dungeon in 1954.

Below: Herstmonceux Castle, East Sussex, c. 1910. Every bit the epitome of a haunted castle, a 9-feet-tall ghostly drummer, is said to straddle the battlements at night, beating a ghastly tattoo.

Above: Leeds Castle, Kent, c. 1900, famous for its black dog that appears as a dreaded omen that someone who lives within the walls of the castle is soon to die.

Below: Rochester Castle, Kent, c. 1900, is haunted by the ghost of the beautiful Lady Blanche de Warrenne who was killed by an arrow that was not meant for her in 1264.

Above: The east terrace garden at Windsor Castle where Guardsman Bentley, 2nd Battalion, Coldstream Guards shot at a ghost in March 1906 (note the elephants).

Below: The gatehouse of Berry Pomeroy Castle, South Devon, c. 1910. Haunted by the spectre of Margaret de Pomeroy, described in the *Weekly Telegraph* in 1936 as 'probably, the most ominous and dangerous ghost in England'.

Taunton Castle, Somerset, c. 1910. The trudge of the Duke of Monmouth's troops killed in battle in 1685 are still said to be heard passing through the castle.

Chapter 4

East Anglia

Life itself is but the shadow of death, and souls departed but the shadows of the living.

Sir Thomas Browne

Bungay Castle, Bungay, Suffolk

Originally built as a motte and bailey by William de Noyers, one of William the Conqueror's stewards, Bungay Castle was bestowed on Norman knight Roger Bigod by King Henry I in 1103. Bigod was awarded several estates in East Anglia and became one of the most powerful families in East Anglia. Roger's son, Hugh, known as Bigod the Restless, was made Earl of Norfolk in 1154 and it was he who would order the construction of the stone keep on the motte. In 1294 one of his descendants, Roger, 5th Earl of Norfolk, was granted a licence to crenellate the castle. After 200 years in the hands of the Bigods, Bungay Castle reverted to the Crown and fell into disuse. In 1312, Edward II gifted the castle to his brother, Thomas Plantagenet, and it eventually passed to the dukes of Norfolk in 1483.

The problem was Hugh Bigod was powerful, but he was not just restless; he was hungry for even more power and got involved in rebellions against the king. According to legend he also became dissolute, was excommunicated for his sins, and his damned soul haunts the castle and its surroundings in the form of a huge and fierce black dog. Bungay has been synonymous with manifestations of demonic black dogs for centuries. Local people and visitors have claimed to have seen the spectral dog well into the twentieth century.

If the black dog was not enough, the Bigods were doomed to ride in a phantom coach too as Morley Adams explained in *In the Footsteps of Borrow and Fitzgerald* (1914):

> The Bigod family seem to have degenerated morally, and the last scions of this mighty house were notorious for profanity and wickedness. Part of the penance is that their unshriven spirits shall haunt the scenes of their earthly sins. In a huge coach, by some stated to be made of leather, and by others wood, they drive abroad on certain nights every year. The coach is drawn by four fiery steeds, from the mouths and nostrils of which proceed flames and smoke.
>
> The ghostly coachman pilots the prancing horses with superb skill, in spite of the fact that often he has to carry his own head under his left arm. The route taken by the Bigods' coach is a clearly defined one; it proceeds from Bungay along the high-road, passes the church, down the lane in which the 'Hateful Thing' is often seen, called Lovers' Lane, and down Bigods' Hill and home again to Bungay by the low road.
>
> One characteristic of this ghostly coach is, I believe, unique. It is never both seen and heard at the same time. Only a few persons, probably those born under the chimes, have seen this strange phantom; but many have heard it. It comes rumbling down Bigods' Hill, the horses snorting and panting; nearer and nearer it comes, and louder and louder grow the sounds of it, until it passes you and the sounds diminish and gradually die away in the distance. To those who have been privileged to see it there is no sound; like a silent wraith the phantom coach glides by, and though the prancing hoofs of the horses strike fire from the ground, no sound is heard. ... Fortunately, no untoward events follow its appearance, and the apparition portends nothing; one trembles to think of the trouble were it otherwise, for so often is it heard that 'unmerciful disaster' would follow.[1]

Burgh Castle, Great Yarmouth, Norfolk

Burgh Castle and its sheltered harbour – probably known as Gariannonum – was large enough to garrison 500–1,000 Roman foot soldiers or up to 500 mounted troops and their horses, such as the Equites Stablesiani cavalry unit from the Rhineland that was based at Burgh in AD 395. Its mighty walls and bastions were once faced with flint and tile. The facings are gone and the west wall has fallen away but large sections of the fort's walls dating from about AD 300 remain today and stand almost to their original height; only the parapet to protect soldiers patrolling the tops of the walls are missing. No other Roman building in East Anglia has survived so well.

In AD 410 the Emperor Honorius withdrew the last of his military units, leaving the occupants of Roman Norfolk to fend for themselves. Rather than falling because of bloody enemy action, many settlements were simply deserted and defences left to rot.

It appears Burgh Castle is haunted by several ghosts. The oldest recorded haunting is the ghostly body that appears wrapped in a large white flag or sheet and is flung from the top of the ruins every year on 3 July. The wrapped body falls but disappears before it hits the ground. Misty figures have been seen in quantity, moving in a body across the ground outside the walls. Although indistinct, it is tempting to suggest these are the ghosts of Roman legionaries marching.

Some of those who have camped in tents overnight within the walls of the castle have reported having the deeply unnerving experience of hearing what they describe as 'the sound of battle, the gallop of horses, the sound of sword upon sword and the cries of the mortally wounded', only to fearfully unzip their tent planning to bolt away to avoid the battle raging around them – and then to be greeted by the silence of the night and not another soul in sight. Disembodied voices have been heard in and around the castle during hours of daylight and at night when nobody else is in sight. Those interviewed about what they heard swore these were human voices, not shouts, just in conversation but too indistinct to understand what they were saying. A large spectral devil dog with burning red eyes, very similar to Black Shuck, known as 'Old Scarfe', has also been seen loping around these ancient ruins.

Caister Castle, Caister near Great Yarmouth, Norfolk

Caister Castle, commissioned by Sir John Fastolf in 1432, is the only example of a Wasserburg castle in the country and one of the first major brick buildings in England. After the death of Fastolf the castle devolved to John Paston. Fastolf's other heirs did not accept Paston's ownership and after years of legal battles, they sold what rights they had to John de Mowbray, the Duke of Norfolk. The Wars of the Roses saw battles breaking out around Britain and the Duke used the war as a vehicle to lay siege to Caister with 3,000 men in 1469. The garrison of thirty men led by John Paston junior held out for two months but after being severely damaged, the castle fell to the duke's men. The castle was eventually returned to the Paston family after the death of de Mowbray in 1476.

The manifestation is said to date back to the Fastolfs and was inherited in turn by the Paston family; it is said to take the form of a spectral carriage drawn by headless horses that appears to warn of the imminent death of a member of the family. In *The East Coast of England* (1861) Mackenzie Walcott noted:

> The peasants believe that at midnight yearly a dark coach, drawn up by headless horses, rolls into the dark courtyard, and carries away some unearthly passengers; a superstition like that of the black headless dog of Mundesley, which scares travellers by night on the lonely coast-side.[2]

Castle Acre, Castle Acre, Norfolk

Castle Acre is a quiet village over in the west of Norfolk. It is probably best known for the picturesque ruins of the priory that provided such a wonderful backdrop for Roger Corman's film adaptation of Edgar Allan Poe's *The Tomb of Ligeia* (1964), starring Vincent Price as the widower Verden Fell, in an iconic costume of the 1820s with top hat and oblong sunglasses with side shades. What Corman may not have known was that the nearby ruins of Castle Acre castle were the scene of what was believed to have been a genuine and very scary haunting in the early nineteenth century.

Castle Acre was founded shortly after 1066 by William de Warenne, 1st Earl of Surrey who fought beside William the Conqueror at the Battle of Hastings. It was built in the centre of de Warrenne's estates in Norfolk near the intersection of the River Nar and the Peddar's Way. During The Anarchy (1135–53), as potential heirs and their supporters scrabbled for the crown of England, the earthworks of Castle Acre were raised, the inner and outer baileys were topped with stone walls and the old hall at the centre was converted into a square keep. Two stone gatehouses were added to the defences in about 1200 and the main road into the village still runs between its flinten towers. By 1397 the castle had fallen into disuse and as it fell into ruins over subsequent centuries, it was used as a source for building materials and rubble for road repairs.

Who or what haunted the castle was not recorded. The only incident that stands out as a possibility, dating from the early nineteenth century, is the tragic case of 'Captain' James Belcham (34) in 1819. Belcham and another man named William Thurrold were brought before the Norfolk Assizes charged with breaking open a room of the Ostrich Pub at Castle Acre and stealing 500 yards of hempen cloth, to the value of £70, being the property of Thomas Smith of Bressingham. Both men were found guilty and sentenced to death, but Thurrold was reprieved and his sentence commuted to imprisonment. Despite Belcham being a Castle Acre man with parents said to have been of 'reputable character', he would not be so fortunate

A curious misunderstanding may just have been the doom of Belcham. He was the head of a gang of river lighters, two barge-like craft that were linked by a huge steering pole fixed to the bow of the second lighter, which extended forward to the cockpit halfway along the leading lighter. The skipper or 'captain' steered the 'gang' using the rear lighter as a rudder.

The problem was, for some reason, the appellation 'Captain' gave the court the impression Belcham was the leader of a gang of depredators in the neighbourhood and because of this misunderstanding he was made an example of by being sent to the gallows on Castle Hill, leaving his heavily pregnant wife a widow and depriving two young children of their father.

Belcham was returned to Castle Acre for burial in the churchyard on the Sunday following his execution; his funeral sermon was heard by a congregation said to be 1,000 strong and was published as a chapbook.

It also presents the possibility that the ghost of Belcham lingered around the ruins of the old castle in the hope of exacting revenge on some of those who had ensured he kept his appointment with the hangman.

The exorcism at Castle Acre was serious enough for not just one but three priests to be called in. The case was related by the antiquary the Reverend James Harvey Bloom (1860–1943), author of *Folk Lore, Old Customs, and Superstitions in Shakespeare Land* (1929) who had been born and grew up in the vicarage at Castle Acre where his grandfather, the Reverend John Hague Bloom, was vicar of the parish church of St James from 1835 to 1873. One of the three priests who carried out the exorcism would have been Reverend Bloom's predecessor, Reverend John Ambrose Tickell. John Harvey Bloom's account was published in *Notes and Queries* (1918) in reply to a question from a fellow reader about the nature of exorcisms:

> The service as performed at Castle Acre in Norfolk, early in the nineteenth century, consisted in requisitioning the services of three of the neighbouring clergy, who read in rotation verses of Scripture, the ghost also reading and keeping pace with them. If the clerics managed to get a verse ahead, their power was established and – the ghost laid. The recess the spirit was put to rest in had two candle-ends thrown in, from which, I presume, they were lighted during the ceremony. My informant, an old lady, aged 84, was present (so she said) when the event took place. The recess was an object of dread in my boyhood. It was securely barred, two wooden bars and an iron one crossing from side to side; but I believe it was merely an opening into a huge chimney stack.[3]

Castle Rising, near King's Lynn, Norfolk

Built about 1138 by William d'Albini for his new wife, Adeliza of Louvain, the widow of Henry I, Castle Rising was far more a home and symbol of power and status rather than a fortress built to defend a strategic position. William was a staunch supporter of King Stephen and helped arrange a truce between the king and Henry Plantagenet that resulted in Treaty of Wallingford which brought an end to The Anarchy (1135–53). When Henry ascended the throne in 1154, he conferred an earldom on William and in turn William remained loyal to Henry during the revolt of Henry the Young King and helped to defeat the rebellion in 1173. The castle was sold to Thomas Howard, Duke of Norfolk in 1544 and remains in Howard family hands to this day. Castle Rising Castle comprises three baileys, each with its own large earthwork covering a total area of five hectares. It remains one of the best-preserved and -decorated keeps in England, surrounded by some of the most impressive earthworks in the country.

Castle Rising, however, is most famous for being where Queen Isabella, 'the She-Wolf of France', lived after her fall following her part in the murder of her husband Edward II at Berkeley Castle in 1327. Despite her misdeeds, Queen Isabella lived her life at Rising in comfort as dowager queen with a suitable retinue of servants. The stipulation was, however, that she should never show her face in public again. Some accounts claim that as time passed the queen became deranged and took to walking the battlements after dark, lamenting her life, wailing for her lover Mortimer who had been executed, and screaming at her fate. The queen was moved to Hereford Castle and died there in 1358, but it was not long after her death that her ghost began to appear at Castle Rising and her eerie screams and hysterical laughter were heard from the battlements once more.

The walls of Castle Rising have seen centuries of history that seem to manifest in paranormal activity. Mysterious mists have been captured on photographs hovering in some of the rooms, there are cold spots, and residual hauntings seem to be replayed there. In a well-attested incident in the early 1980s a mother and her son (11) both saw a woman and child in 'medieval' clothes pass close by them holding her toddler's hand as it made its way down the tall steps of the castle. When the visitor mother asked a member of staff outside if a reenactment or special event was due to take place, she was told they had no special events on that day and there was no one is costume in the castle; the mother and son had had the place to themselves.

Apparently, the member of staff did not appear surprised at the enquiry, nor did she make any joke of it. In fact, it was as if people had approached her after similar occurrences on previous occasions. Enquiries and research by the author at Castle Rising over the years have confirmed this was almost certainly the case and many people have apparently glimpsed moments from the past replayed at Castle Rising.

Colchester Castle, Colchester, Essex

Colchester Castle has a fascinating history. The building seen today is a Norman castle that dates from the second half of the eleventh century, built on the foundations of the Roman Temple of Claudius. If you have the chance, travel down and see the lower levels under the keep, where even the layer where Colchester was burned to the ground by the Iceni during the Boudican revolt in AD 60–61 can clearly be discerned. The most dramatic of the hauntings in the castle date to the seventeenth century and the turbulent years of the English Civil War.

In August 1648 Colchester was held by Royalists and was besieged by Parliamentary forces under Sir Thomas Fairfax. After weeks of misery the Royalists had no other option than to surrender. The Royalist leaders Sir Charles Lucas and Sir George Lisle were taken outside and just to the rear of the castle where they were to face a firing squad. Sir Charles declared, 'See, I am ready for you; and now, rebels, do your worst!' Sir George kissed his dying friend farewell and asked the musketeers to come a little closer. One of them replied, 'I'll warrant ye, sir, we'll hit you.' Sir George smiled and replied, 'I have been nearer you when you missed me.' Rising from his prayers, he cried, 'I am now ready; traitors do your worst.' A memorial to these brave gentlemen now stands where they were executed.

Their ghosts, resplendent in their cavalier uniforms with magnificent hats have been seen in the grounds, near the Lucas vault and on the great staircase where they have been seen descending the stairs; they pass straight through the metal gates, turn right and disappear through the thick wooden doors that lead outside.

During the sixteenth and seventeenth centuries hundreds of men and women were accused of malevolent actions and even murder by witchcraft across East Anglia. The worst period of persecution was undoubtedly during the witch scares and persecutions when Matthew Hopkins, the Witchfinder General, was active during the 1640s. In one instance in 1645 some thirty-five women from Manningtree and surrounding villages were brought to Colchester Castle, the county prison at the time, where they were imprisoned and interrogated by

Hopkins and his team. They were then held in the cells until they faced trial; some fourteen of these women would be found guilty of witchcraft and were sent to the gallows as a result.

The Reverend John Gaule expounded his criticism of Hopkins, his assistant Stearn and other witch finders, publishing tracts exposing their greed, ignorance and methods, declaring them worse symbols of rebellion and chaos than the witches upon which they made war, and his conviction and abhorrence that:

> Every old woman with a wrinkled face, a furrowed brow, a hairy lip, a gobber tooth, a squint eye, a squeaking voice or scolding tongue, having a rugged coat on her back, a skull-cap on her head, a spindle in her hand and a dog or cat by her side, is not only suspect but pronounced for a witch.

Gaule's voice of reason was not alone and underpinned a complaint that forced Hopkins to answer some challenging questions posed by the judges at Norwich. Hopkins protested his motives were both godly and sincere and claimed he had been the victim of malicious rumours. Some of those accused of witchcraft were held in the cells at Colchester Castle as they awaited trial. Reverend Gaule exposed the methods of Hopkins and his team used on accused witches when in custody:

> Having taken the suspected witch, she is placed in a room upon a stool or table cross-legged, or in some other uneasy posture, to which if she submits not she is then bound with cords; there she is watched and kept without meat or sleep for the space of 24 hours for within that time they shall see her imp come and suck [witches were said to have a 'devil's tit' with which they supposedly suckled their familiars; to find this a suspected witch could be stripped and 'searched' using a bodkin to prick for areas insensible to pain where the tit was allegedly hidden] … A little hole is likewise made in the door for the imp to come in at: at least at night come in some discernible shape, they at watch are taught to be ever and anon sweeping the room and if they see spiders or flies to kill them. And if they cannot kill them, then they may be sure they are imps.

The cells under Colchester Castle are unspoilt since the time of Hopkins, in fact they are a lot cleaner than back then, but they are very atmospheric. Ghostly presences of those accused of witchcraft have often made themselves known over the years with manifestations, misty human form and disembodied voices, moans and cries of the pain that they suffered all those years ago.

Framlingham Castle, Framlingham, Suffolk

Originally built as a Norman motte-and-bailey castle, Framlingham Castle was destroyed by Henry II after the revolt of 1173–74. The replacement structure consisting of a stone curtain wall, thirteen towers and no central keep, built by Roger Bigod, 2nd Earl of Norfolk, was completed by 1213 and is pretty much the castle that can still be seen today.

The castle was besieged and successfully taken by King John in 1216. By the end of the thirteenth century, the castle had become more of a hunting lodge. By the end of the sixteenth century Framlingham Castle had fallen into disrepair and was given to Pembroke College in 1636. Most of the internal buildings inside the castle walls were subsequently removed to make way for the construction of a poor house built in 1729 on the site of the medieval great hall.

The castle and the buildings within have, on occasion, rung with the laughter of children and the sounds of children playing within the walls long after all visitors and children have gone home. Spectral black boots with no visible person in them have been spotted on the stairs leading up from the bake house and children's faces have been spotted gazing out blankly from the attic windows. The ghostly footsteps, according to local tradition, of a man whose name has been lost in the mists of time, who was imprisoned in the prison tower and subsequently died, are said to be heard making his final walk through the postern gate into the tower before his death.

Occasionally the chilling disembodied screams of a woman have also been heard in the old workhouse. Research by the author suggests the screams may be those of Mary Larter who was brought to Framlingham Workhouse 'in a bad way' in October 1767. The poor woman had clearly been both terrified and physically attacked. On arrival she simply sat for about three hours until she asked her friend Mary Fiske to take her to bed where she died sometime later. The horrifying stories Mary Larter told before she died of the events leading up to her death left her friends in no doubt of the cause of her demise.

Days before, while churning butter at her Master Sherman's house where she was employed, she told her mistress she felt so ill she could not carry on, upon which her mistress insisted she carry on 'even if she dropped down dead'. After finishing the churning Mary collapsed in a faint. The following day her master hit her with her mistress's riding whip because he thought she could milk faster. The following day her mistress pushed her so hard against the pump it caused her nose and mouth to bleed. Unable to get up when ordered, her mistress got her riding whip again, dragged her along screaming as she went and when she managed to get up, he whipped her again. Carried to the magistrate, her treatment was brought to the notice of the law. When the inquest into her death was called the jury was left in no doubt and delivered the verdict of 'Murder by Employers'.

English Heritage staff have voted Framlingham Castle to be one of the top ten spookiest sites.

Hadleigh Castle, Hadleigh, Essex

Hadleigh Castle was founded around 1215 by Hubert de Burgh, chief minister to King John. Quarrels between de Burgh and the king led to his lands and the castle being returned to the Crown in 1239. Around 100 years later Edward II began to use Hadleigh Castle as a royal residence. When it passed to Edward III, he saw the castle's strategic value for the defence of the Thames Estuary against French raiders and saw to it that the castle was extensively fortified during the Hundred Years' War. The castle became a well-loved residence of Edward's in later life. After his death it was rented out to tenants and was eventually sold off in the sixteenth century. A lot of the castle was stripped out and demolished for building materials but there is enough left the make the journey to see it and the landscape that surrounds it worthwhile.

According to local legend the ruins are haunted by a demon or even the Devil himself who is described by those who have seen the manifestation as the 'Black Man,' an entity blacker than night. There is also a ghost known as 'Woman in White'[4] who tries to compel anyone she encounters to dance with her. Who she was or why she the haunts the ruins seems to have been lost over the years. It should also be borne in mind that these stories of the haunting of the ruins of Hadleigh Castle may have been somewhat enhanced in the early nineteenth century by either the wily Essex smugglers who operated in the area or the excise men who used one of drum towers built by King Edward as a lookout.

That said, the ghost of the 'Woman in White' has been spotted gliding among the ruins in comparatively recent years. The demonic black figure has not been reported for many years, but it is intriguing that there have been reports of a huge, frightening black dog with red, glowing eyes and a mouth that foams and slavers. It is possible that one of the spectral devil dogs well known across East Anglia may have wandered to the ruins or it would not be the first instance of the Devil or demon changing its manifestation into a fierce black dog 'with eyes that burn like the coals of hell'.

Kimbolton Castle, Huntingdonshire, Cambridgeshire

The original Kimbolton Castle was built by Geoffrey Fitz Peter, 1st Earl of Essex, in the late twelfth century. In the late fifteenth century, the inner court was rebuilt by Anne, Duchess of Buckingham. Sir Richard Wingfield purchased the castle in 1522, and successive generations of the Wingfield family reconstructed the medieval castle as a Tudor manor house. The castle was sold to Sir Henry Montagu in 1615. He was created Earl of Manchester in 1626, and the castle remained the family seat until 1950, when it was bought by Kimbolton School.

Catherine of Aragon, first wife of Henry VIII, arrived at Kimbolton in May 1534 after Henry had divorced her. Catherine was clearly not of the same opinion as the king, nor did she acknowledge the legitimacy of his actions. She continued to refer to herself as Henry's only lawfully wedded wife and England's only rightful queen consort and her loyal servants continued to address her by that title. Catherine was in poor health; modern medical experts suggest she was suffering from cancer, but she lived with the suspicion that she was being poisoned under the orders of Henry.

Catherine spent the last months of her life as a semi-prisoner in her rooms in the south-west corner of the castle attended by a few of her faithful servants. She fasted for most of the time and only left her quarters to attend Mass; she took to wearing the hairshirt of the Order of St Francis as she prepared to meet her end.

Catherine died at Kimbolton Castle on 7 January 1536. She was buried in Peterborough Cathedral as a Dowager Princess of Wales, not a queen. Henry was not present at her funeral; he also forbade her daughter Mary to attend. The ghost of Queen Catherine is said to have been seen gliding along the corridors and galleries of Kimbolton. In one account from the 1860s it describes the perambulations of Catherine's ghost:

> They say she glides about after dark, robed in her long white dress, and with the royal crown upon her head, through the great hall, and along the corridor to the private chapel, or up the grand staircase, past the Pelegrini cartoons.[5]

Her spirit, however, is believed to favour the chamber where she died to make her appearances. If she is not seen, it has often been claimed her presence can be felt. In his book, *My Candid Recollections* (1932), William Angus Drogo Montagu, 9th Duke of Manchester, recalled:

> An old servant of patriarchal aspect, was convinced that he could talk to her and would break off with an 'Excuse me, your Grace' and bow low to the empty air, repeating her imaginary commands.[6]

His lordship also wrote of the other ghost said to haunt Kimbolton Castle, Justice Sir John Popham (1531–1607). Popham had been appointed Solicitor-General in 1579; in 1581 he was elected Speaker of the House of Commons and was appointed Attorney-General later that same year. In 1592 he was appointed Chief Justice of the Queen's Bench, a position that he retained until his death.

Popham was not known for his leniency; in fact, he was feared for his strict enforcement of the penal laws. He was what would be known as 'a hanging judge' and was never one to shy away from sentencing those convicted to suffer the full rigour of the law.

Justice Popham was involved in the trial of Mary, Queen of Scots for treason at Fotheringhay Castle in 1586, which resulted in her being beheaded. In 1595 Popham presided over the trial of Robert Southwell, a Roman Catholic priest of the Jesuit Order who wrote numerous popular religious tracts. His crime was to have administered sacraments according to the rite of the Catholic Church, the problem being the country had split from Rome and was a Protestant country where no other church would be tolerated other than the Church of England. Southwell swore he had not 'entertained any designs or plots against the queen or kingdom' but he was convicted of high treason and Popham passed the dread sentence upon Southwell whereby would be hanged, drawn and quartered.

Popham also presided over the trial of Sir Walter Raleigh who would be beheaded in 1603. He will probably be best known for presiding at the trial of the eight surviving conspirators of the Gunpowder Plot, including Guy Fawkes, in Westminster Hall on 27 January 1606. Found guilty of high treason they were all hanged, drawn and quartered.

Popham is believed to have lived in Kimbolton Castle around 1600. The Popham Gallery above the chapel is named after him, and his portrait has hung in the house of many years. It seems he was just a ruthless in his home life as he was in court. Local legend tells of how Popham had desperately wanted his wife to produce him a son and heir but after she gave birth to a daughter, he hurled the baby from an upstairs window onto the courtyard below, killing her instantly. Even if the story is untrue, I think it is a reflection upon the regard with which Popham was held by the people of the estate and surrounding area.

The ghost of Sir John Popham is said to sit astride the park wall of Kimbolton Castle; he is said to wander the estate and lies in wait for rogues and poachers under the great elms. The 9th Duke of Manchester wrote of Popham's ghost:

> From the books of the period, it is doubtful whether the haunting is done in a contrite spirit, and more probable that the excellent judge is still incensed at his failure to obtain his desire, the inheritance of the Montagu estate.[7]

Norwich Castle, Norwich, Norfolk

Norwich Castle was begun shortly after the Norman Conquest of 1066 when an area of land was cleared, defensive ditches were dug and a wooden fort erected atop a great mound. Work was begun on a stone keep in 1094 by King William Rufus and was continued after his death by his brother, Henry I. Norwich Castle was completed by 1121. Designed more as a royal residence and a symbol of power rather than a fortification, it has spent the greatest part of its life as the county gaol, a role it served from the fourteenth century until 1883, when the prisoners were removed to the new prison off Plumstead Road and work began on converting the ancient castle into a museum, a purpose it serves to this day.

Over the last 200 years staff, inmates when it was a prison, and visitors to Norwich Castle have reported occasional sightings of a ghostly woman dressed in a long, black early nineteenth-century dress. It is highly likely she is the ghost of Martha Alden who was hanged in front of a huge crowd on the gallows outside Norwich Castle on 31 July 1807.

Martha had ended up there because her husband, Samuel Alden, preferred to lie in bed rather than get up and go to work. The couple lived in a cottage in Attleborough and one day Martha, 'seized with a sudden mania', hacked Samuel to death with an agricultural billhook. Martha called upon her neighbour and friend Mary Orvice to help her hide the body which they put into a corn sack, hid in it the garden then carried it under the cover of darkness to the pond on the common and 'shot' it into the water.

The concealment of Samuel Alden's body was clumsy and his body was found floating in the water soon afterwards. Tried at the Norfolk Assizes, Mary Orvice was lucky to escape the gallows with a stern warning from the judge, but Martha Alden was found guilty of murder and faced the full rigour of the law. The judge 'doomed her to death, to be drawn on a hurdle to the place of execution, there to be hanged by the neck, and her body to be dissected'. Martha went to the gallows, dressed in the mourning black of a widow, and after she had been hanged, her body was passed to the surgeons.

A ghostly figure identified as Martha Alden was seen walking abroad on Norwich Castle mound soon afterwards. News of this reached Attleborough and a party of men set out for Norwich in December 1807, armed with bell, book and candle determined to hide out on the mound and lay Alden's ghost to rest if it appeared. A problem arose when as the group waited: watching time tick by, they started taking a nip or two of spirits of their own while waiting for the ghost to appear. As the hours went by, they obtained further supplies from the nearby Bell Inn and this group of ghosthunters became roaring drunk and very rowdy. They were seized by the gaoler and held in the prison for two days pending an enquiry into their conduct.

The ghost of Martha Alden was never laid to rest and has been seen on numerous occasions ever since. In one notable incident in 1820 complaints were lodged with the gaoler by prisoners after they had been 'terrified half to death' by a manifestation of 'something indescribable' which passed over them as they slept in their beds during the small hours of the morning.

It is believed that the ghostly figure dressed all in black that disappears around corners in the art gallery areas of the castle where the old cells used to be is the ghost of Martha Alden. After the execution of Frances Billing and Catherine Frary, the infamous 'Burnham Poisoners', for the murder of Billing's lover's wife and Catherine's husband in 1835, they too were said to haunt the castle mound, gliding up towards the castle from the site of the gallows near the entrance lodges.

Wandlebury Ring, Cambridgeshire

Some of the oldest haunted castles and sites are to be found in East Anglia, and this tale comes from what is probably the oldest haunted location in this book and is one of my favourite ghost stories. Wandlebury Ring was first settled in the fifth century BC, fortified and enclosed by wooden ramparts, with two ring ditches added around 400 BC. This Iron Age hillfort was inhabited by the ancient British tribe of the Iceni. Ancient human remains have been found in the Ring Paddocks, in Varley's Field. Another field just outside the hillfort is believed to have been an Iron Age cemetery.

Wandlebury Ring stands on the edge of the Gog Magog Hills, a landscape redolent of ancient mysteries, for here there are stories of ancient giants, forgotten gods, rituals, ley lines and chalk imagery that is believed to have been carved onto the hillside centuries ago. The site was later occupied by the Romans. In 1685 King James II had a racing stable built in the hillfort that was acquired by Francis, 2nd Earl of Godolphin in the 1730s. Here he built a substantial house, laid out beautiful gardens and expanded the racing stables. The house was demolished in the 1950s but many of the other buildings remain and there are pathways and fields open to the public today.

The legend attached to Wandlebury Ring recorded by Gervase of Tilbury in *Otia Imperialia* in the early twelfth century tells of how, if a knight dared to enter the Ring by moonlight and cried 'Knight to knight, come forth', a ghostly night-rider would appear, do battle and the victor could claim a prize of their choice. Whichever knight unseated the other would be the victor.

One knight who did not wish the challenge to go unmet was Sir Osbert FitzHugh who called forth the Night Rider at Wandlebury Ring by moonlight. After a fierce exchange Sir Osbert gained an advantage, unseated the Night Rider and knocked him to the ground. As victor of the contest Osbert claimed his adversary's steed. The infuriated Night Rider threw his lance at Osbert and disappeared. Osbert carried off the horse and displayed it in Cambridge. Like the knight, it was black with black trappings but at cockcrow it broke loose and just like the knight it also disappeared. Sir Osbert was left a reminder of his fight with the Night Rider. The lance he threw at Osbert only delivered a glancing cut to his thigh and it was quick to heal but every anniversary of his fight with the Night Rider the wound would open up again as if fresh, would bleed profusely and then heal again immediately.

Woodcroft Castle, Etton, Peterborough, Cambridgeshire (formerly Northamptonshire)

Woodcroft Castle is privately owned and is not open for public visits, but it was the scene of one of the most brutal killings during the English Civil War and a consequent haunting that should be included in any book on haunted English castles. It began as a fortified manor house the thirteenth century but most of its defences date from the early Tudor period. At the time of the English Civil War, it stood as a good, strong property, surrounded by a moat that would have at least stood a chance of holding out against a siege. At least that is what Dr Michael Hudson (1605–48) had hoped.

Hudson was a man of God and on the outbreak of the English Civil War, he had joined the Royalists. He fought at the Battle of Edgehill in 1642 and retired afterwards to Oxford where he was introduced to King

Charles I; he must have made a good impression too for he was soon made one of the royal chaplains and received a Doctor of Divinity in 1643.

King Charles appreciated Hudson's frankness; he certainly pulled no punches, so the king dubbed him his 'plain dealing chaplain' because he 'told him his mind when others would, or durst not'.[8] Hudson was also most certainly a fighting chaplain and a brave leader. He toured Norfolk and Suffolk in 1648 recruiting troops for the Royalist cause. Hudson was in the process of taking his reinforcements to support King Charles at Stamford but was headed off and cornered by Parliamentarian forces under Colonel Thomas Waite. Hudson and his men fell back to Woodcroft Castle and took refuge while Waite and his larger force laid siege to the castle. In less than forty-eight hours the Roundheads forced the doors of the castle and made their entry on 6 June 1648.

The Royalists had fought bravely and only yielded on the promise of being given quarter but as soon as they had surrendered, the Roundheads reneged on the deal. Hudson and the last of his men made a fighting retreat to the roof where Hudson was flung over the battlements. As he fell, he managed to catch hold of a waterspout on the guttering and desperately tried to cling on, only for the Roundheads to chop his hands off with swords and he dropped into the moat. Fearing he would drown Hudson asked that he be allowed to die on land. Dragged out of the water Hudson was then delivered a fatal blow to the head with the butt of a musket by a soldier named Egborough, while another soldier named Walker, a chandler or grocer in Stamford, cut out Hudson's tongue 'and carried it about the Country as a trophie'.

The *Athenæ Oxonienses* notes the fates of Hudson's killers:

> Egborough, he was not long after torn in pieces with his own gun, which burst while it was under his arm in Long Orton; and Walker since, through poverty, quitted his trade, and was become a scorn and by-word to the boys when he passed through the streets of Stanford [*sic*].[9]

Hudson's ghost is said to still haunt Woodcroft Castle; locals would occasionally hear his shouts and screams for mercy and his handless spectre dripping moat water and blood still showing every wound that took his life wanders the banks of the moat on the anniversary of his death.

Chapter 5

London

With her head tucked underneath her arm
She walks the Bloody Tower
With her head tucked underneath her arm
At the midnight hour.

Stanley Holloway

The Tower of London

The earliest known haunting occurred when King Henry III was reinforcing defences and adding more cells to the Tower. When, as the work was nearing completion, according to the chronicler Matthew Paris in his *Chronica Maiora* (1241) on the night of St George's Day, 1240, the foundations gave way and all that had been built was reduced to rubble. The work was restarted, and in a year, it was again nearing completion when it fell overnight yet again. The paranormal cause of the demolitions during the hours of darkness were, at least according to Paris, revealed to a priest in a vision who saw a venerable figure:

> an archbishop, dressed in bishop's robes and carrying a cross in his hand, came to the walls which the king had built at that time at the Tower of London and, after regarding them with a scowling look, struck them strongly and violently with the cross, saying 'Why do you rebuild them?' Whereupon the newly built walls suddenly fell to the ground, as if thrown down by an earthquake. The priest, frightened by this, said

> to a clerk who he saw following the archbishop, 'Who is this?' To which the clerk replied, 'It is St Thomas the martyr, a Londoner by birth, who considered that these walls were built as an insult and to the prejudice of the Londoners, and has therefore irreparably destroyed them.'

Becket had been dead nearly a hundred years, and Henry III felt the retribution for his grandfather's ordering that he should be 'rid' of Becket that resulted in Becket's murder, being visited upon him. Paris would record how on another occasion when another loss was suffered by the king, he exclaimed, 'Woe, woe is me. Is not the blood of the blessed martyr Thomas fully avenged yet?'

The new works carried out at the Tower included a chapel dedicated to St Thomas Becket in the royal quarters and the tower on the Thames became known as St Thomas's Tower. The water-gate beneath it, originally intended to be a royal entrance to the Tower became associated with prisoners such as Anne Boleyn and Sir Thomas More who were brought by barge to the Tower and became known as Traitors' Gate. Perhaps Becket does not like that nom de plume so closely situated to the parts of the Tower that bear his name and it has been suggested that the ghostly sound of monk's sandals on wooden floors heard even in areas that are carpeted may just be Becket making himself known.

The spirit in St Thomas's Tower, whoever it may be, is not a destructive one. Major-General Sir George Younghusband, the Keeper of the Regalia, would recall when he was living there a solid door in his dressing room had a habit of opening and shutting silently when nobody was anywhere near and there was no breeze in the building.

The earliest monarch whose ghost haunts the Tower is Henry VI, who was murdered in the Tower in 1471. Where and how he was murdered in the Tower is debated; some point to a killing on the orders of Richard of Gloucester (later Richard III). Originally buried in Chertsey Abbey in Surrey, Richard ordered Henry be removed to St George's Chapel, Windsor Castle in 1484. When Henry's body was exhumed from his tomb in 1910, he was found to have an abnormally thin skull that had been badly damaged. Whether the damage had been caused through his murder or in the process of exhumation and reinterment was unclear to the experts of the time. The unseen phantom hands that have attempted to push staff and guests downstairs are associated with the death of

Henry; his ghost is said to appear in the Wakefield Tower on the stroke of midnight.

Richard's bloody hands are also involved in the next haunting, one of the most famous, the Princes in the Tower. The uncrowned Edward V (12) and his brother Richard, Duke of York (9) were placed in the Tower in 1483 by their uncle, Richard of Gloucester. While in the Tower the princes were declared illegitimate and Gloucester usurped the crown to become King Richard III.

To secure his throne Richard is believed to have ordered Sir James Tyrell to make the young princes disappear. Tyrell arranged and oversaw John Dighton his horsekeeper and Miles Forrest, one of four Tower guardians of the princes, to suffocate the boys with pillows and hide their bodies in the Tower. It is claimed that when under sentence of death for treason in 1502, Tyrell finally confessed to his heinous deed.

In 1674 workmen at the Tower uncovered a wooden box under a staircase leading to the chapel of the White Tower that was found to contain two small human skeletons. The bones were believed to be those of the princes. King Charles II had them buried in Westminster Abbey. Their ghosts, wearing nightgowns and walking hand in hand, linger around the Bloody Tower where they were imprisoned and probably murdered. They have been spotted playing on the battlements and the giggling of young children around the Tower late at night when there are no youngsters around is believed to be the princes.

Anne Boleyn (1507–36) is probably the most famous ghost at the Tower of London; she even had a music hall song written about her haunting. Anne was the second wife of King Henry VIII, and presented him with a fine daughter (who became Elizabeth I) but produced no male heir so Henry decided to dispose of her. He had her arrested, imprisoned in the Tower and tried on trumped-up charges of treason and adultery. Anne was convicted on 15 May and executed four days later, on 19 May 1536. Anne had seen the mess made by executioners at the Tower, so she requested that she be beheaded by a sword wielded by one of the far more experienced headsmen from Calais. The king graciously granted her wish.

On 19 May Anne was escorted to Tower Green, just to the west of the White Tower where she mounted the scaffold. She then removed her headdress and tucked her hair under a coif. After bidding farewell to her weeping attendant ladies and a request for prayers, she knelt upright; one of her ladies tied a blindfold over her eyes and she uttered her final prayer in which she continuously repeated: 'Jesu receive my soul; O Lord God have pity on my soul.' As she did so the executioner got his assistant to make a noise, Anne instinctively looked to the sound, turning her swanlike neck to the executioner and with one deft sweep of the sword, she was decapitated.

Her body was placed in a narrow chest and buried in an unmarked grave in the Chapel of St Peter ad Vincula within the walls of the Tower. Anne has walked the corridors and grounds of the Tower ever since. Usually seen after dark, Anne appears close to the site where she was executed. In one infamous incident in the year 1864 on a freezing cold winter's night, Tower Green and the white stuccoed house called the Lieutenant's Lodgings were bathed in moonlight of an unnatural radiance. As the relief guard neared the house which is in the south-west corner of the inner walls, the corporal peered into the shadows cast by the trees. There was no sign of the sentry who should have been at his post. Puzzled, the corporal raised his lantern and only then did he spot him. The sentry lay sprawled on the cobbled pavement, his eyes closed and his face white in the moonlight. He lay practically under the window of the room in which Anne Boleyn is believed to have spent her last night.

'Asleep at your post,' muttered the corporal to himself. 'You're for it, me lad!' But the sentry of the 60th Rifles was not asleep. He had fainted and a few days later he would give his own account of what had happened at a court martial for what initially appeared to be his unmilitary conduct. We are fortunate to have the recollections of Captain, later Major-General., J. D. Dundas and Lieutenant, later Field Marshal, Lord Francis Grenfell to draw on for an account of the extraordinary story to which the sentry swore was the truth about what had happened to him.

He said he had been standing sentry at his post near the Lieutenant's Lodgings, reckoning that there was not much more of his two-hour spell to go when a white figure suddenly appeared before him He challenged the figure but received no reply and raised his bayonet, but his bayonet passed right through the figure. Asked what happened then, the sentry replied, 'Then, sir, I must have fainted.' The sentry was then asked to tell the court what the figure was like? He replied, 'It was the figure of a headless woman.' You would probably expect the court to be incredulous of his claims – there was certainly unsympathetic laughter – but two other soldiers had happened to look out of the window of their room in the Bloody Tower before going to bed and had seen a white figure approaching the sentry at his post quite distinctly and in the moonlight. They had heard him issue his challenge as it carried clearly through the still night air and they had seen him collapse after he lunged at the figure. Their evidence, and the unshakable story of the sentry himself, was enough to convince the court and the soldier was acquitted.

The ghost of Anne has been seen on many subsequent occasions too. William Ewart Nicholls, a former sergeant in the Artist's Rifles would recall:

> I was at the Tower of London in the very early hours of a day in 1915, when a spy was to be executed. The moon was at the full, and I was on sentry duty. We had just changed the guard when the officer on duty said, 'What is that woman doing here at this time of the morning?' We turned our heads and saw distinctly in the strong light the form of a woman moving rapidly across the Square towards the wall near the river, and before we could sufficiently recover ourselves to take any action she had disappeared through the wall (which I believe at that spot is 9ft. thick!). We learnt afterwards from one of the warders that it was the ghost of Anne Boleyn, who had previously appeared before a death in the Tower.

In his book *The Tower of London from Within* (1918) Major-General Sir George Younghusband noted: 'The most haunted spot, apparently, is where [the] sentry stands, the door of the Lieutenant's Lodgings under the window leading into Queen Anne Boleyn's room.'

In February 1933 a sentry at his post near Martin Tower believed he saw the ghost of Anne Boleyn and fainted. The warders and their wives at the old fortress were described in the press as 'humming with stories of this latest visitation'. One account of what happened stated:

> A sentry was patrolling near the magazine when he heard piercing scream. He ran towards the spot, and discovered that a young soldier, also on sentry-go, had collapsed.

> The guard was called out, and the sentry was found to be incapable of carrying on. He maintained in the face of strict questioning by superior officers that he had seen with overwhelming horror the shadowy figure of a headless woman approaching. Mistrusting his vision in the darkness he challenged the figure. There was no reply. The rifle with its bayonet fixed fell from his hands and with a scream he fell unconscious.

The women who lived in the official quarters in the Tower at the time firmly believed that Anne 'walked'. One of them told a reporter:

> she has frequently seen a shadowy figure glide across the green in the shadow of the White Tower and the Bloody Tower. The figure was startlingly like the pictures she had seen of Anne she said, 'It moved slowly and sadly along. I could not find it in my heart to be frightened of the poor soul.'

The article went on to add:

> In recent years a number of young soldiers stationed in the fortress have sworn to seeing apparitions. They have not been overlooked as the authorities who realise that sentry-go in the grim shadows of the Tower imposes a strain.[1]

An officer of the guard was making his rounds one night in the 1870s with either the Corporal or the Sergeant of the Guard when he saw that a light was burning in the Chapel of St Peter ad Vincula. As it was after midnight and the door of the chapel was locked, any question of a service being held was impossible.

The officer called for a ladder to enable him to look through a window. According to his story he found the whole of the interior of the chapel illuminated by a bluish light in which he could see a procession of men and women. They were dressed in Tudor clothes and were walking slowly down the aisle. At their head walked an elegant figure of woman with jewels in her hair whose face was averted from him, but whose form the officer said he recognised from portraits as Anne Boleyn.

When asked later if he wasn't very much surprised or alarmed, the officer said that he wasn't in the least and: 'It was only when the light suddenly faded and I found myself standing rather foolishly at the top of a ladder peering through a window at utter darkness that I realise the people couldn't have been real.'

Margaret Pole, Countess of Salisbury, was 67 when her execution took place on Tower Green on 27 May 1541. Her execution was a reprisal for the actions of her son Reginald Pole, Cardinal Archbishop of Canterbury, who had drawn the wrath of King Henry VIII for his denunciation of Henry's creation of himself as Supreme Head of the Church of England, and for the king's divorce from Catherine of Aragon. The cardinal had gone to France and was out of reach of the king, so Henry vented his spleen upon the cardinal's family instead and threw them into the Tower. Henry reserved the cruellest punishment for the cardinal's mother, not least because she had been born a Plantagenet and Henry suspected anyone of that dynasty of having designs on the throne.

The countess languished in the Tower for two years until a date for her execution was set. This poem was found carved on the wall of her cell:

For traitors on the block should die;
I am no traitor, no, not I!
My faithfulness stands fast and so,
Towards the block I shall not go!
Nor make one step, as you shall see;
Christ in Thy Mercy, save Thou me!

The Countess of Salisbury's execution would be just the sort of beheading that Anne Boleyn had dreaded. A low wooden block had been prepared for her execution on Tower Green instead of the customary scaffold. When she faced her executioner, the countess refused to place her neck on the block saying: 'So should traitors do, and I am none.' The countess would not be still either, Lord Herbert recorded: 'turning her grey head every way, shee bid him if hee would have her hedd, to get it off as best he could; so that he was constrained to fetch it off slovenly.'

The problem was the chief executioner had been despatched to the north to deal with rebels, and the execution was performed by 'a wretched and blundering youth who hacked her head and shoulders to pieces in the most pitiful manner'. One story tells of how the countess ducked away as the executioner raised his axe and he chased her around the block, hacking at her until she died a gory death. Another account tells of how the first fall of the axe missed her neck and gashed her shoulder instead. Chased or not, witnesses agree it took eleven blows of the axe for the executioner to silence her and finally part her head from her body. The countess was buried in the Chapel of St Peter ad Vincula. Her ghostly blood-curdling screams are said to be heard occasionally echoing around Tower Green; visitors have even claimed to have seen a ghostly replay of the chase.

The king who damned the countess to such a horrific death would in turn haunt the Tower too. In 1890 a sentry was on duty in the Beauchamp Tower when he thought he heard his name being called. Turning round to face where the voice came from, he was confronted by 'a red bloated face, with a loose, dribbling mouth and heavy lidded pale eyes' that seemed to be floating in mid-air. The sentry recognised the visage from paintings he had seen to be that of Henry VIII himself! Perhaps it is also the ghost of King Henry who inflicts the terrible crushing sensation occasionally experienced by guards and visitors when entering the hall where his impressive suit armour is exhibited.

In 1553 as the young king Edward VI fell gravely ill, he planned who should succeed him in the event of his death. Rather than his half-sisters, Mary and Elizabeth, whom he considered illegitimate, he named his cousin Lady Jane Grey as his successor. His half-sister Mary and her supporters had other ideas. On the death of Edward, Jane's father-in-law John Dudley, the Duke of Northumberland sought to enforce the king's wishes and marched with a small body of troops to capture Mary but surrendered on receiving the news the Privy Council had changed allegiance and proclaimed Mary as queen. Mary would become known as 'Bloody Mary' for her persecutions and executions and Northumberland would be one of the first of her reign of terror. Convicted of high treason for attempting to place Lady Jane Grey on the throne, he was beheaded on Tower Hill on 22 August 1553. The ghost of the duke has been seen strolling between the Martin and Constable towers; sentries named the pathway 'Northumberland's Walk'. He walked abroad one night in 1969 when a distraught sentry rushed to the guardroom gibbering 'man in a cloak, man in a cloak!' and had to be treated for shock before he could say that the ghostly figure he had seen was headless.

'Bloody Mary' would also see to it that the uncrowned Jane was thrown in the Tower charged with high treason, along with her husband, two of his brothers, and Thomas Cranmer, the Archbishop of Canterbury. All were found guilty and sentenced to death. Lady Jane was sentenced 'to be burned alive on Tower Hill or beheaded as the Queen pleases'.

On 12 February 1554 Lady Jane watched her husband Lord Guildford Dudley going to his execution from the window where she was imprisoned in the house of Master Partridge, the Tower's Gentleman Gaoler. She then saw Guildford's body and decapitated head delivered to the chapel by cart. Jane became distraught and recovered her composure just in time for her to be led to the scaffold. Jane's husband had been beheaded in front of a huge crowd on Tower Hill. Jane had the small mercy of her execution being granted the comparative seclusion of Tower Green.

Fearing some instant fall of the axe she implored the executioner: 'Will you take my head off before I lay down?' The tall, masked executioner reassured her he would do nothing until she was ready. She bound her own eyes with a kerchief but then panicked, reaching her arms out for the block she exclaimed' 'What shall I do? Where is it? Where is it?' One of her ladies guided her neck onto the block, weeping as she did so. Jane then spoke her final words: 'Lord, into thy hands I commend my spirit!' The axe then fell and with one blow he decapitated the queen of nine days. Lady Jane Grey was just 16 years old. She was buried with her husband in the chapel of St Peter ad Vincula.

The ghost of Lord Dudley has been seen sitting in his cell in the Beauchamp Tower weeping late into the night The white figure of Jane is said to haunt the battlements of the Tower. One of the most notable sightings of the ghost of Lady Jane was made by two sentries who spotted her running along the battlements of the inner wall close to the Salt Tower just after 3 a.m. on 12 February 1954, the 400th anniversary of her execution. Exactly three years later to the day two Welsh Guardsmen saw what they described as a 'white, shapeless form' in a similar location. The paintings of Lady Jane are far less known than those of Anne Boleyn so the ghostly figure of a young, graceful, woman, 'suffled in white' that has been seen on numerous occasions around the Tower, with and without a head or face, may also be Lady Jane Grey.

Explorer and statesman Sir Walter Raleigh was imprisoned in the Tower by both Elizabeth I and James I and would spend over 13 years in the Bloody Tower. On his final stay in the Tower he would be held the Beauchamp Tower before he was beheaded outside the Palace of Westminster in 1603. His ghost has been encountered on the staircase inside the Bloody Tower and along the battlements in a section that has become known as Raleigh's Walk. In 1976 the wife of one Yeoman Warder was alone in their battlement house when she distinctly felt a hand brush her back as she bent over her bath, built where the doomed Sir Walter Raleigh once walked as a prisoner. The stoical woman was nonplussed and exclaimed: 'Oh, stop it, Raleigh!'

Guy Fawkes, the most famous member of the 'Gunpowder Plot' to assassinate James I by blowing him up during a visit to Parliament in 1605 was thrown into the Tower where he was imprisoned in the Queen's House. When questioned, Fawkes refused to name his fellow conspirators. He was then subjected to torture on the rack in the White Tower dungeons to extract the names from him. For half an hour he bore the agony then his fortitude gave way, and in feeble voice he promised to tell all. The shaky hand of Fawkes signed his name to his confession. Sentries and visitors alike have reported they have heard the phantom cries of Fawkes's agony as he was tortured, muffled by the immense thickness of the walls, proceeding from dungeons of the White Tower. His cries and groans have also been heard from the dreaded cell known as 'Little Ease' where Fawkes passed his last days, a place so small that the prisoner could neither stand upright or at full length, its occupant forced to keep in a constant cramped position.

Another famous ghost of the Tower is that of Arbella Stuart who haunts the Queen's House on Tower Green. Arbella was once seen as a potential successor to Queen Elizabeth I, but it would be her marriage to William Seymour, Duke of Somerset, the nephew of Lady Jane Grey that would seal her fate. The marriage did not have the permission of King James I who considered the union a threat to the Crown. Consequently, Seymour was imprisoned in the Tower and Arbella in Sir Thomas Perry's house in Lambeth. The pair managed to plot an escape, but Seymour missed the ship on which he was meant to flee to the continent with Arbella.

Seymour sailed soon afterwards and made it to Flanders but the ship carrying Arbella was intercepted by another carrying some of the king's men just before it reached Calais. Arbella was returned to England, and she was imprisoned in the Queen's House at the Tower. There she began to refuse to eat, fell ill, and died on 25 September 1615. Some would claim she was murdered by being starved to death. Those who have encountered her ghost claim that initially she appears solid enough, her colouring natural but pale but if she moves or is observed for some time it becomes apparent she is quite transparent and features of the room behind her can be seen through her; then she just melts away as if she was never there.

One of the best-attested paranormal manifestations in the Tower occurred in the early nineteenth century. Mr Edmund Lenthal Swifte was the Keeper of the Crown Jewels from 1814 till retirement in 1852. He was a highly regarded man of some distinction, who played a courageous part in saving the regalia during the terrible fire which destroyed the Armoury in the Tower in 1841. No one privileged to know him could have questioned the honesty with which he related his story, which he recorded with his absolute 'pledge of faith and honour' that all he recorded he had seen with his own eyes. The events occurred when the regalia in his charge was at the time kept in the Martin Tower, which forms the north-east angle of the Inner Ward, and where he had rooms with his family:

> One Sunday night in October 1817, I was at supper with my wife, our little boy and my wife's sister in the sitting-room of the Jewel House, which is said to have been the 'doleful prison' of Anne Boleyn, and of the ten bishops whom Oliver Cromwell piously accommodated there. ... The room, irregular shaped, had three doors and two windows cut 9ft. deep into the outer wall, between these a chimney piece projecting far into the room and [then] surmounted with a large oil picture. On the night in question the doors were all closed, heavy dark cloth curtains were let down over the windows, and the only light in the room was that of two candles on the table.
>
> I sat at the foot the table, my son on my right hand, his mother fronting the chimney-piece, and her sister on the opposite side. I had offered a glass of wine and water to my wife, when on putting it to her lips she paused, and exclaimed: 'Good God! What is that?' I looked up, and saw a cylindrical figure, like a glass tube, seemingly about the thickness my arm, and hovering between the ceiling and

> the table; its contents appeared be a dense fluid, white and pale azure, like to the gathering of a summer cloud, and incessantly rolling and mingling within the cylinder. This lasted about two minutes, when it began slowly to move before my sister-in-law, then following the oblong shape of the table, before my son and myself, passing behind my wife, it paused for a moment over her right shoulder (there was mirror opposite in which she could then behold it).
>
> Instantly she crouched down, and with both hands covering her shoulder, shrieked out: 'Oh, Christ! It has seized me!' Even now while I write I feel the fresh horror of that moment. I caught up my chair, striking the appearance with a blow that hit the wainscot behind her. It then crossed the upper end of the table and disappeared in the recess of the opposite window. Neither my sister-in-law nor my son beheld this appearance.

As a result of this bizarre manifestation an additional sentry was accordingly posted outside the Martin Tower in case someone or something should return. Mr Swifte continued:

> Following hard at heel on the visitation of my household, one of the night sentries at the Jewel Office was, as he said, alarmed by a figure like a huge bear issuing from underneath the door. He thrust at it with his bayonet, which stuck in the door, even as my chair dinted the wainscot. He dropped in a fit and was carried senseless to the guard room. His fellow-sentry declared that the man was neither asleep nor drunk, he himself having seen him the moment before awake and sober. Of all this I avouch nothing more than that I saw the poor man in the guard house prostrated with terror, and that in two or three days the fatal result, be it of fact or fancy, was that he died.

The unfortunate soldier was buried with full military honours in the Flemish burial ground at St Katharine's by the Tower. Mr Swifte was writing of these events decades after they happened and while I am sure his recollection of the events themselves were vividly etched in his memory, they may well have taken place the year before. The *National Register* published in London on 14 January 1816 was one of several newspapers to report the following story:

> For some weeks past, a family residing in the Tower of London have been very much annoyed and disturbed by a variety of unpleasant and strange noises heard in different parts of the house during the night; and the sentries on duty at the door of the Royal Regalia, to which this house belongs, have frequently been disturbed by the most violent knocking, and (according to their account) even deep and hollow groans have been heard; and the feeling of superstition having spread very much among the soldiery, with whom the ghost is now a cant phrase, an additional sentry has lately been placed on the rampart immediately over the mysterious spot, and every possible exertion used by the occupier of the house towards elucidating the cause of the disturbance.
>
> Officers of the garrison have watched for whole nights; nothing but a continuance of the noise was heard but no visible cause discovered, until late on the night of Thursday last, the inhabitants of the Tower were thrown into the greatest possible confusion, by the screaming and roaring of the sentry stationed at the door of the Regalia depot, and the turning out of the guard, which, upon repairing to the spot, found the soldier extended on the pavement in a senseless state.
>
> He was immediately carried off to the guard room, and, when sufficiently restored to his senses, positively affirmed, that whilst upon duty, a small figure crept from under the door at which he was stationed, and gradually made its approach to him, at the same time changing its appearance to that of a human being, and afterwards into that of a dog. These sudden transformations so completely affrighted the soldier, that, after alarming the whole neighbourhood with his bellowing, he fell down senseless. Nothing was seen by the soldier placed on the rampart; and the most rational conclusion is, that imbecility of mind has in this

> case been worked upon by the ridiculous and absurd tales of 'the ghost', with which, most probably, the poor fellow's weak brains have been crammed; and certainly no rational person can say that doubling the sentries for such reasons as in this case tends much to assure the uneducated mind of such lunacies …

These events prompted the recall of a bizarre event two decades earlier. The *Carlisle Patriot* of 27 January 1816 reported the following as fact:

> We understand that about twenty years ago a similar alarm prevailed in the Tower, upon the presumed appearance of a ghost in nearly the same spot the sentinel of that day on duty was missing, and the next morning was apprehended at Turnham Green as a deserter. The account which he gave of himself was, that a spirit had caught him up in its arms and carried him through the air; and that all that he recollected of his voyage was, that in passing over St Paul's church, he struck the cross with his heel. The spirit, however, did not attend the Court Martial to substantiate this statement, and the man was sentenced to, receive, and did actually receive, 300 lashes as a deserter.

Could this really be a case of a soldier from the Tower being snatched away by a paranormal entity? Perhaps, a precursor of the Spring Heel'd Jack incidents of the late 1870s or even what may be described in more modern times as an alien abduction?

He may not have been the last soldier in the Tower to find himself somewhere he did not expect to be either. In the early hours of Wednesday 22 February 1928, Coldstream Guardsman Frank Ricardo (21) had been in the Guards just 11 months when he was found by a sentry lying in his night attire at the bottom of the moat at the Tower. Ricardo had no idea how he had got there. He was sent at once by ambulance to the Queen Alexandra Hospital, Millbank where he was found to be suffering from several injuries: his wrists were broken, his nose injured and his side was bruised. His mysterious appearance in the moat was blamed on Ricardo, variously, having fallen from the battlements, steps or a 15-feet-high window while walking in his sleep. No explanation was offered for how he appeared to have remained asleep during and after his fall – even when he sustained his injuries.

Another bizarre occurrence took place on the night of Saturday 25 March 1854. The *Berkshire Chronicle* recorded:

> The Tower of London was thrown into some confusion, owing to the nervousness of a young recruit. About 12 o'clock the sentry posted at the back of the Jewel house was heard screaming in a frightful manner. Colonel Wyndham, the Keeper of the Jewels, jumped out of bed. Other sentries of the guard ran immediately to the assistance of the man, whom they found nearly paralysed with fear and his firelock on the ground. He was immediately relieved and taken to the guard-house, where he gave the following story: – 'That as St Paul's clock was striking 12, a figure approached him, whom he instantly challenged, but receiving no answer he challenged a second time, and so it approached nearer and nearer towards him. It grew in size, until he thought it reached the moon.' The poor fellow got into such a nervous state the sight of the monster, that it was some time before he recovered.

The 1920s and 1930s were decades when many sightings of ghosts were made by visitors and sentries at the Tower. Tragedy struck when Guardsman Alfred Bembridge (23) of HQ Company, 1st Battalion, Scots Guards was found dead by the corporal of the relief at 2 a.m. on Tuesday 8 April 1924 at his sentry post at the magazine, a single sentry post eighty yards from the guardroom. He had died from a single shot to his head. His service rifle was lying near him, found to have recently been fired but no one had heard a gunshot. Guardsman Bembridge had been in the Guards for over two years; he was well liked and his comrades recalled how he had been laughing and joking about his equipment before he went on sentry duty that night. Nothing had seemed untoward.

At the inquest Sergeant Collier stated, 'Bembridge had been a most excellent man until about three weeks ago when I noticed a change in him.' Collier added that he 'understood that some months ago Bembridge had some trouble with a young woman and other people had written to him worrying him about money.' It all seemed very vague. Bembridge had recently written to his parents stating he would be leaving the army in August when he had served his term. The coroner recorded a verdict of deceased 'took his life while of unsound mind'. Some of Bembridge's comrades believed that he had 'seen something' while on sentry at the Tower, that what he had seen had haunted him and he was never the same again.

In early December 1930 the headless ghost of the Duke of Northumberland who had been executed in 1553 walked again. A young Guardsman saw it and refused point blank to mount guard at the same spot again. In the end the authorities tacitly accepted his refusal, did not punish him and gave him guard duty elsewhere.

The story reached the ears of investigative reporter Gideon Clark who went to experience a night in the Tower for himself in December 1930. Clark's article is wonderfully evocative; the author of this book has also had the privilege to be a guest after dark when the public have gone home and can confirm the atmosphere of the Tower that Gideon describes has changed little in nearly a hundred years:

> While the roar of the City traffic can plainly be heard and parties of smiling visitors, dressed unmistakably in the style of 1930, crowd about one, the rumours headless apparitions and sobbing Queens seem fantastic and unreal enough. It is a very different matter to visit the Tower, as I did, towards midnight in winter, when the wind howls dismally about the battlements, and the whole place is a mass of eerie shadows. The gloom of the grim walls is emphasised by darkness and silence, and their terrible memories take on new life as a sleeper relives his past in a dream.
>
> At ten o'clock the Tower closed for the night. First the outer wooden gate that opens on Tower Hill, then that of the Middle Tower, then the Byward Tower gate are solemnly and ceremonially locked. The keys are carried, escorted by soldiers, through the Bloody Gate handed into the custody of the Governor of the Tower, an officer representing him, by means of an ancient ritual which was recently broadcast.
>
> Posterns are left open in all three gates, but at eleven these are closed, and after that hour it is only possible enter or leave the Tower by giving the password, which is changed

each day. After three in the morning, it is impossible for anyone to enter or leave the Tower under any circumstances whatever. Officers who have been detained in town or in the country have to spend the rest of the night in their cars or else stay in a hotel.

Towards midnight the Tower grows absolutely silent. Only the footfalls of the sentries guarding the Crown jewels in the Wakefield tower – the millions of pounds' worth of gold and glittering gems – and their occasional challenge can be heard. Now is the time for ghosts! Walking across the stilled and deserted Green, where the Queens, Anne Boleyn, Katharine Howard, Jane Gray, were beheaded, one remembers suddenly that they were buried in the little church not 20 yards away. One remembers, too, that the tiny diamond-paned window in the Beauchamp tower immediately above is the one from which Lady Jane Grey saw the bleeding corpse of her husband brought back from execution.

A mere historical fact in the daytime but now – something painfully real and haunting! Dim lamp-light flickers upon the windows of the church which encloses so much tragic dust, and for an instant, a pale and lovely face seems to peer from one of its panes. Is that a sigh that passes or is it night-wind only?

So one comes by dark, winding stairs to the place, high among the battlements, where the Duke's ghost is said to have been seen. It is a walk, once used by prisoners of rank, from Martin's tower to the Constable's tower. The feet that once so restlessly paced it have gone away. All is silent as the grave.

Did I see the ghost? I saw shadows and felt them. I became aware of all the Tudor and Stuart dead close about me, and of the tragic life which once moved and breathed about those stones. I saw something move in the darkness. It may have been nothing – nothing at all …[2]

During the Second World War, the Tower of London, along with the rest of the East End, suffered bombing during the London blitz in 1940. Several buildings in the Tower were destroyed or damaged by high-explosive bombs, including parts of the Mint and the Old Hospital Block. Stretcher-bearer parties rescuing wounded from buildings reduced to ruins and rubble and became a familiar sight but one night a sentry on the main gate of the Tower reported he had seen a procession of uniformed men advancing and carrying a stretcher with a body and its severed head. Their uniforms they were wearing, however, were nothing like those he was used to seeing and they faded into the darkness only a few yards away from him, leaving the soldier shocked and confused. On the sentry's report an investigation was ordered. The uniforms he described the strange procession were wearing were found to match those worn by medieval sheriff's men who brought executed corpses back to the Tower for burial.

During the war the last execution of a German spy by firing squad would be carried out at the Tower. Josef Jakobs had landed by parachute on farmland near Ramsey, Huntingdonshire in the early hours of 1 February 1941. He had broken his ankle on landing and was still sitting in the field in his jump suit with his parachute behind him when a couple of smallholders found him and alerted the Home Guard. They handed him over to the police and in turn Jakobs was placed in the hands of the relevant military authorities and was taken to Brixton Prison Hospital Infirmary for treatment for his broken ankle.

When interviewed in due course by Lieutenant-Colonel William Edward Hinchley-Cooke of MI5 he freely gave his name as Josef Jakobs and confirmed he was a German citizen and stated he was to send reports back regarding weather conditions. Jakobs was charged under the Treachery Act on 24 July 1941. Hinchley-Cooke read over the charge to him in German and Jakobs replied, 'I have nothing to fear.'

Josef Jakobs was tried before a general court martial held at the Duke of York's Headquarters, King's Road, Chelsea on 4–5 August 1941. Found guilty as charged, Jakobs was removed to the Tower of London and was held in a cell at Waterloo Barracks until Thursday 14 August 1941 when he was escorted to the miniature rifle range that stood between the Constable Tower and Martin Tower in the Outer Ward of the Tower of London. There he was seated in a brown Windsor chair, blindfolded and a piece of white lint pinned over the area of his heart as an aiming patch for the eight-man firing squad drawn from members of the Holding Battalion, Scots Guards. At 7.12 a.m. the squad opened fire and Jakobs was no more.

The body of Josef Jakobs was quietly removed to St Mary's Roman Catholic Cemetery, Kensal Green where he was buried in an unmarked grave. The Windsor chair with the section blown out of the backrest by the well-grouped shots bear mute testimony to the accuracy of the firing squad and is now on display in the White Tower, The chair is displayed in a glass case but the energy experienced by those open to such things when they stand near it is, I am told, palpable and understandably very dark. The miniature rifle range has been taken down and removed but the ghostly figure of a man dressed in a 1940s suit is still occasionally seen around the Outer Ward. He has only been known to appear since the execution and is believed to be spectre of Josef Jakobs. Another ghost joins the cavalcade of history at the Tower.

There are other nameless spirits too. A presence has been reported by occupants of the Constable Tower, the home of a Yeoman Warder and his wife. The presence is said to return regularly and is heralded by a strong smell said to be like that of the compounded odour of leather and sweating horse flesh that attaches to a horseman who has been riding hard. The spirit seems friendly enough, but one Warder's wife claimed the ghost once nudged her arm so strongly when she was writing that her pen jolted across the paper. The figure of a man dressed in medieval attire and the uncanny sound of footsteps on the stairway happened so frequently one night that when the figure was seen and heard, residents from the upper floor followed the footsteps down the stairs; those living on the ground floor heard them too and came up the stairs only to meet each other in the middle.

A dark entity warders described as 'the nameless thing' has been known to terrify those guarding the Tower as they walk their beat from the River Thames Sally Portal entrance. Stones have been thrown by invisible hands. In 1968 another terrified sentry had to be relieved of his duty when he was found alone but gasping: 'They're following me up and down on my beat.' A Guardsman on sentry reported a sensation of someone throwing a cloak over him. When he tried to free himself, the cloth was seized from behind and pulled tightly around his throat by the invisible attacker.

Chapter 6

The South East

The thing came to a standstill only a few yards from me, but apparently the first shot made no impression, so I reloaded, and fired straight at it. The bullets must have gone clean through the ghost.

Guardsman Bentley

Arundel Castle, Arundel, Sussex

Arundel Castle has only ever been in the hands of two families since it was built by Roger de Montgomery, a cousin of William the Conqueror, in the eleventh century. In 1555 it passed by marriage to Thomas Howard, 4th Duke of Norfolk and remains in their family to this day. Besieged during the English Civil War in 1643, the Royalist garrison surrendered after eighteen days. The castle was then slighted by order of Parliament. Arundel Castle was restored, remodelled and embellished during the eighteenth and early nineteenth centuries by successive generations of the Duke of Norfolk.

Ghost and paranormal activity has been seen and experienced in numerous locations inside and out at the castle but it is best known for five distinct hauntings. The ghost of young girl in white has been seen in the vicinity of Hiorne's Tower where it is said that having had her heart broken, she threw herself from the battlements. She seems to prefer dusk as a time to appear near the brow of the hill where the tower stands. Sadly, her name had not been passed down with the story nor a date for of the tragedy. The sounds of Cromwell's cannon fire during the siege have also been heard hammering the walls of the castle.

The magnificent castle library is haunted by the ghost of a seventeenth-century cavalier. Usually seen at night, he is beautifully dressed in blue silk doublet and breeches. Known as 'the Blue Man', he seems to be silently searching for a book he can never find. The library is also haunted by a little black dog seen more by children than adults; room stewards have often been asked about it and must explain there is no little dog in the room. It is believed to have been the pet of Philip, 13th Earl of Arundel (1557–95) who was imprisoned in the Tower of London during the reign of Elizabeth I for refusing to renounce the Catholic faith. Howard was not executed for fear of him becoming a martyr, but he died while being held in the Tower. He was later canonised by the Catholic Church as St Philip Howard.

The castle kitchens are believed to be haunted by the tragic figure a boy scullion who was grossly mistreated; some even say he was 'worked to death' many years ago. The sound of him hard at work cleaning and tidying has been heard on many occasions but he is rarely seen. When he does appear the ghost of the boy is seen working his heart out at the sink.

Betchworth Castle, Brockham, Dorking, Surrey

Betchworth Castle began as an earthwork fortress in the eleventh century. Granted to Richard FitzAlan, Earl of Arundel in 1373, his son Sir John FitzAlan built a stone castle on the site in 1379. It passed to Sir Thomas Browne, Treasurer to the Household of King Henry IV and Sheriff of Kent in 1448 who rebuilt it as a fortified house. Most of crumbling ruins seen today date from Browne's house with later developments built between the sixteenth and eighteenth centuries.

The spectre said to haunt the ruins and their grounds (now Betchworth Golf Course) has been dubbed 'Lord Hope,' but the haunting may well predate the time when the Hope family owned the Castle. The story behind the haunting tells of how a previous owner of the house had been made responsible for the safekeeping of a political prisoner at the castle. One night the prisoner escaped and 'Lord Hope' and the men of his retinue set off in search of the fugitive.

Arming himself with a sword, 'Lord Hope' went to investigate and encountered a figure in the darkness sooner than he expected and called on him to stop but the figure failed to do so. 'Lord Hope' took no chances and ran him through with his sword. Calling for the servants to bring a light 'Lord Hope' discovered to his horror that he had killed his own son whom he had failed to recognise in the darkness and in his haste. The ghost of the penitent father still walks the ruins wracked with regret.

The ghost was still being seen in the late twentieth century. John Walker, a former curator of Dorking Museum, told the story of how when he was a child, he had encountered the ghost of 'Lord Hope' when he was out with his mother. Mr Walker recalled 'the figure looked like a man lamenting, bent over saying, 'Oh God, what have I done?' He was not ashamed to admit on seeing and hearing the spectre that he and his mother clung to each other and they hurried away.

Bramber Castle, Bramber, Steyning, West Sussex

Only one remaining 14-metre-tall fragment of the tower wall hints at the stronghold that one stood on this site. Bramber Castle was constructed shortly after the Norman Conquest on a natural knoll to defend a gap in the South Downs and give a command over the nearby estuary of the River Adur. Held by William de Braose, 1st Lord of Bramber, it would remain in the hands of the de Braose family for many generations, except for a short period when it was confiscated by King John (1199–1216).

The William de Braose who owned the castle at the time had a full and opulent lifestyle that was envied by the king. He would also to incur the king's displeasure in the events leading up to the signing of the Magna Carta in 1215. King John decided to make an example of Braose and ordered him to give up his four young children as hostages of the king to ensure ensuring their father would behave in the future.

Braose refused the demand, so King John despatched some of his troops to Bramber to take the children by force. Braose got wind of the king's actions and fled to Ireland with his family. They did not evade capture for long and were escorted back to England where they were imprisoned at Windsor Castle. While they were there, King John saw to it that the four Braose children starved to death as a warning to other barons. It is the wizen little ghosts of these four children 'all dressed in rags' who return to haunt the ruins of Bramber Castle and the nearby road to the village, especially at Christmastime, when they appear to beg for food, but if anyone should speak to them, they just disappear.

The castle is also said to be haunted by a pair of tragic lovers who died at the castle during the time of the English Civil War. There is also the folktale which tells of the son of a Lord of Bramber who fell in love with a pretty servant girl, but she preferred a local boy. When she turned down the young Lord's invitation to attend Bramber Fair with him, he ordered the girl to spread manure on a nearby field before she would be allowed to attend the fair.

Suddenly the Devil appeared – he always tries to get you when you are down – and he made the offer that he would help the girl if she gave him a kiss. The girl was taken aback but she knew by the time she had finished the dirty and smelly work on the field, she would be in no state to go to the fair, so she agreed to the kiss in payment. Lo! The job was done but 'Old Nick' wanted more but thank goodness the girl's boyfriend came to her rescue; however, the Devil said he would return to claim what was due to him.

The young couple sought the advice of the vicar of Bramber. The old cleric told the girl to tie a bundle of hay round her foot at sunrise when the Devil was next expected. This the girl did and when the Devil appeared, he seized the hay as a forfeit. As he grasped at it the hay seemed to grow in size until it there was one almighty rush of wind that carried away both the hay and the Devil until they disappeared out of sight and the Devil returned to Bramber no more.

Chilham Castle, Chilham, Kent

Chilham Castle was built by Sir Dudley Digges in 1616 on the site of a medieval castle. Chilham Castle is now a luxury retreat hotel, but it was well known to be haunted by the ghost of the 'White Lady' for many years before when it was nothing more than a very grand family home with no interest in attracting visitors. One of the few times a group was given the privilege of a visit to the property over the years was when it was the home of Lord and Lady Killearn; the Whitstable Historical Society were greeted and shown around personally by Lady Killearn in September 1949. The local press covered the visit and although the house had 'an imposing interior', works of art, historic portraits and many fascinating things to see, it was noted 'the ghost failed to put in an appearance'.[1]

The legend of why the White Lady haunts the castle tells of how she had been a member of the household of Lord Bartholomew de Badlesmere, who had owned Chilham Castle in the fourteenth century. For some misdemeanour his lordship had her bricked up in the dungeon walls. Perhaps she had cursed Lord Batholomew for some reason, for he had the bad judgement to support what proved to be an unsuccessful rebellion to depose Edward I, led by Thomas, 2nd Earl of Lancaster. Lord Bartholomew was tried and found guilty of treason at Canterbury and was hanged, drawn and quartered at Blean in April 1322. After his execution his head was displayed on the Burgh Gate at Canterbury.

The White Lady would, however, make some dramatic appearances on other occasions. Chilham Castle was being used for location filming for *The Amorous Adventures of Moll Flanders* (1965), directed by Terence Young and starring Kim Novak, Richard Johnson and Angela Lansbury (we will all know Dame Angela from her portrayal of the murder-mystery-author-turned-detective Jessica Fletcher in the long-running and much-repeated TV series *Murder She Wrote*). Our story involves Kim Novak, lead actor in the title role of the film, who was shooting a scene in the castle when she saw the ghost of the White Lady on the dungeon stairs; she was given such a fright that she fell down the stairs and was badly shaken by the experience. She was off work for some time as a result.

In 1974 Chilham Castle was then kept by the Lord Massareene and Ferrard and Mr Alex Jardine, who employed Mr Roy Neeve as the manager for the medieval dinner parties that were being held there on a regular basis at the time. Mr Neeve encountered the 'White Lady' one night when he was clearing up after a dinner; he told a *Maidstone Telegraph* reporter:

> I was leaving the Regency Room on the way down to the Dungeon Bar when I heard a violent flapping. I thought someone had forgotten to close a window and turned to it. Then I saw the ghost. It was not so much a figure, more a sort of misty brightness! There was no doubt about its eerie quality. I was scared, stepped back a sharp couple of paces, fell downstairs, and went to hospital for four days with a badly sprained ankle.[2]

Mr Alex Jardine and his son Charles pointed out that neither of them really believed in ghosts but admitted that something strange was going on at the castle. Charles recounted one incident when he was working in the Gold Room at the top of the keep when he heard a sudden crash in a cupboard:

> At the same time the windows flew open. My dalmatian dog Jay was scared to death. Now he will not go near the place. Lord Massereene's Alsatian is another animal which puts up its hackles whenever it is brought near the keep and then refuses to budge.[3]

In August 1974 Jenni Balow visited Chilham Castle during her research for her Haunted Kent series of articles published in the *Kentish Express.* She spoke to Debbie (her surname was not given), one of the banquet minstrels who had encountered the 'White Lady' at the top of a flight of stairs. All the staff wore medieval costumes for the dinners and Debbie thought there was nothing unusual about the pale young woman passing her who did not reply when Debbie spoke to her, but she got a shock when she looked again and the woman had disappeared. The only place she could have gone was through an 8-foot-thick wall.

By August 1974 Mr Alex Jardine had to admit it is not difficult to imagine that the castle was haunted, especially 'when the moon is full, and the castle is silhouetted against the sky, and dog foxes are barking in the park, it is not difficult to sense a presence around the place'. He had also witnessed things he could not explain, as the feature explained:

> he was standing in the Lucius Room in the Keep. He watched a vase full of flowers lift off a window ledge and travel on its own at eye level across the room. Finally it stopped suspended in mid-air and then crashed to the floor. His reaction was to feel "numbed' at the sight. The story is backed up by the fact that another member of staff saw exactly the same thing happen on another occasion.[4]

He assured the reporter that he would be keeping a very open mind to paranormal phenomena from then on.

Dover Castle, Dover, Kent

Dover Castle has sat atop the White Cliffs guarding the shores of England for centuries and is one of the most iconic of all English fortresses. Founded in the eleventh century, the stone keep, the walls of the inner bailey and parts of the outer curtain wall were built by Henry II between 1179 and 1188; this magnificent castle is rightly known as the 'Key to England'.

The castle was Royalist at the outset of the English Civil War, but it was captured by Parliamentary forces soon afterwards. From the 1680s to 1749 it was used to hold French prisoners of war. The defences of the castle were strengthened, and a new barracks was built as Britain prepared to defend its shores from invasion by the French during the Napoleonic Wars (1803–15). The finest hour of the castle was to come in May 1940, when deep in the maze of old tunnels under the castle Admiral Bertram Ramsay and his team became the nerve centre controlling Operation *Dynamo*, the evacuation of thousands of troops from the beaches of Dunkirk.

The walls of Dover Castle exude history; you really can feel history happened within them and there have been many instances of paranormal activity there over the years from cold spots and full apparitions to phantom smells and poltergeist activity. With so many ghosts and so much history, it seems many of the spirits are transient: they are seen or experienced only once or twice and then they are gone. In the tunnels underneath the castle there have been numerous instances of residual replays from the Second World War ranging from the noises of activity in an operations room or hospital area when there is nobody in the rooms and no display films or soundtracks are playing, to a uniformed soldier walking purposefully up one of the narrow tunnels when visitors have stepped aside to let him pass only for no one to go by.

The place in the tunnels where the most frequent sightings have been reported is in the repeater station where a ghostly Royal Navy officer appears to be checking instruments at the far end; then having carried this out, he walks towards where the public stop to view the area from behind barriers. The ghost, who often appears quite solid, walks through the barrier and disappears out of the room. Several members of the public have been very taken aback by the sight of this ghost during tours over the years.

When the author was involved in some of the events to commemorate the fiftieth anniversary of the D-Day landings at Dover Castle in 1994, a soldier in Second World War uniform was occasionally seen in the barrack rooms after hours. No one ever got close enough to talk to him; he was just there one minute and then he was gone without anyone seeing him leave. A few people had the same experience and questions were asked about who he was, but he was not known to be a member of any of the reenactment groups present for the event.

One night the sound of soldiers singing barrack-room ballads was heard distinctly near the keep by the author and several other members of his group. The songs were being sung clearly enough for some of them to be recognised as those dating back to the First World War that were sung again by troops during the Second World War, along with some of the songs with really unrepeatable lyrics that soldiers sang in the latter conflict, but the group of soldiers who were singing them could not be found. There was nothing eerie about it at all. We felt honoured to hear them and we raised a glass to those lads … wherever they were.

Those serving in the forces like to play pranks on one another. Ghost stories get spun just like lamps can be swung and pity the poor sentry who hears the 'phantom footsteps' that have been built up by the stories of his mates or the ghostly figure of a comrade draped in a white sheet appears to float by in the dark. I will leave it up to you to make up your own minds about the following two stories.

The first was published in the *Dover Express* shortly after the publication of *Turn Over the Page*, the reminiscences of Sir Lionel Earle, a career civil servant who had served as Permanent Secretary at the Office of Works, 1912–33 His chief claim to fame was to have been the senior continuous-serving official in the Office of Works, and over the years after the First World War, he had a great deal of influence in the creation of London's war memorials. Page was certainly not a man prone to flights of fantasy. In his book Sir Lionel tells the story of an ex-air force officer who on hearing the keep of Dover Castle was haunted, obtained permission to spend the night there, but had to agree to the doors being locked as was usual practice at the time. It was undoubtedly one of the first recorded 'paranormal lockdowns':

> Six in the morning the Keep was opened and he was found white as a sheet and speechless and was an hour before he

> could say anything. When asked what had happened, he related that at ten o'clock he had gone to bed and shortly fell asleep. How long he had been asleep he did not know, but he was awakened by what sounded to him like the tramp of an army in rubber shoes. He sat up in bed and listened. Suddenly from one of the Norman passages leading into the big chamber a white lady appeared. He spoke to her and asked her if she was in trouble and whether there was anything he could do for her. She did not reply but passed on and went out by another Norman passage the other side of the room. It seems strange that this episode should have completely knocked out a man who had never known fear. He said he would not sleep there again for a million pounds.[5]

The second story is probably the one ghost of Dover Castle that has become more notorious than any other. The ghost of a drummer boy from the Napoleonic Wars is said to walk above and below ground at Dover Castle at full moon. The story first hit the press during the last year of the Second World War and has been told many times since. Here is the story told in the *Kentish Express* in 1958:

> Peter Watkins was drummer boy to Dover Garrison. His job was to walk round the turrets and ramparts of the castle to tap out drum messages that ordered the comings and goings of the military. It also was his job to go to headquarters to collect the garrison pay.
>
> On one of these occasions, he was returning through some underground passages when he was set upon by ruffians. It was a cleverly planned attack, the legend has it, and within a few moments Peter lay headless upon the ground, his hand clutching a shred of the bag containing the payroll. A great hue and cry was set up but to no avail – the culprits remained free.
>
> Now Peter is alleged to wander the ramparts and the underground passages, beating out a ghostly rata-tat upon his drum, in search of his head. Nobody can claim to have met him although his existence is never denied. The only proof of any ghostly manifestation comes from the last

> century when a young lieutenant of the Guards decided to wait one night to see the headless drummer boy.
>
> He descended into the dark and dank dungeons and there lay in wait. The next morning searchers went to look for him – they found him stark mad with his dark curly hair turned overnight into a brilliant white thatch. Nobody ever heard from him what happened during that fateful night. If anybody should know about Peter. it should be old Harry Leeming, for years Custodian of the Castle. He knows the old legend but has never seen Peter. 'Some nights in my home in the tower I have heard a ghostly tapping, but I have never discovered what it was caused by,' he says.[6]

Back in 1945 the story of the phantom drummer even appeared in the national papers. The serious army with a serious job to do in 1945 did not want to get involved in any notions of a phantom drummer boy appearing at Dover; when asked for an official comment, Brigadier Cecil Whitefield Raw, Deputy Constable of Dover Castle dismissed it all as 'Piffle!'[7] In an effort to add weight to this opinion reporters tracked down those who had served at Dover in the past and asked them if they could recall any sightings or even stories of the drummer boy when they were at Dover Castle and none of them could say that they had heard of it before.

That said, not all ghosts have a long history of manifestation. Any good paranormal researcher knows that if ground is disturbed, demolition work takes place or building work is carried out in an old house, paranormal activity can be triggered. During the Second World War Dover was part of the south-east coast of Britain that had become known as 'Hellfire Corner'. Not only had it been subjected to regular bombing by enemy aircraft, but it had even been shelled by the German long-range artillery on the coast of France. There were also heavy artillery batteries around Dover which fired back too. Dover was a front-line town. If there was any time in its history that a ghost was going to be rattled into activity at Dover Castle, the Second World War was the time it would most likely happen.

I am sure many of the paranormal researchers reading this will have had their investigations disparaged and even prevented at a location by a property owner or manager even though they haughtily exclaim that they did not believe in ghosts. With that in mind, take heart, when it was reported in the press that Sergeant Harry Leeming of the Castle Garrison of the Royal Artillery and a pal from the Royal Navy were going to sit in the passageway at Dover Castle where the phantom drummer was believed to walk, from the rise of the full moon on the night of 27 February 1945 until dawn the following day, with only the light of a pocket torch to await the appearance of the ghost. Just as they were going to set off, they learned that the Castle was closed to them and there would be *no* waiting for the ghost.[8]

Before departing from Dover Castle, I must take you on a brief diversion to the nearby village of St Margaret's that was thrown into panic after a number of women had been terrified by a startling manifestation, perhaps even the notorious Spring Heel'd Jack himself, in November 1904. Some local ghost hunters were determined to do something about it. I came across the story while researching this book and found it so incredible that if it had not appeared in newspapers, I think I would have dismissed it as a tall tale. The story was published under the headline of 'Ghost Hunt: Men in Women's Clothes as Decoys':

> Amusing incidents have occurred in connection with the hunt for a ghost in the neighbourhood of the village of St Margaret's, near Dover. Some of the searchers had declared their intention of 'making it hot' for the ghost, but on one occasion, at least, they fled at the sight of the supposed spectre.
>
> A tall lady went out in nurse's attire on Thursday night. She was dressed in white, and as it was foggy she threw over her head a white shawl. By several persons the lady was taken to be the ghost, and they rushed off, panic-stricken. The nurse's recital of her experience caused considerable amusement for her companions.
>
> A novel way to stalk a ghost was hit upon last night. As his unwelcome attentions have been devoted chiefly to the gentler sex, a band of young men dressed as woman went out to act as decoys. The hunters included a large number of persons who went over from Dover especially to join the chase.

> One contingent claim that the 'Spring-heeled Jack' narrowly escaped capture at their hands on Thursday night. Across some fields they chased him, but when close upon him he was lost to sight in the fog.
>
> A formidable revolver was displayed yesterday by one excited hunter, who, it was understood, had expressed the determination to test, if he had the opportunity, whether the disturber of the public peace was a genuine ghost or composed of flesh and blood.
>
> Practical joking has its serious side. The sight of the ghost springing from behind a hedge startled a horse in a trap on St Margaret's Road, and the driver narrowly escaped a serious accident.[9]

Hastings Castle, Hastings, Sussex

The ruins of the keep and bailey of Hastings Castle stand on the high ground of the town of Hastings overlooking the English Channel. It was one of three castles – Hastings, Pevensey and Dover – ordered to be built by William the Conqueror immediately after his successful invasion in 1066. Originally constructed as a wooden motte-and-bailey castle, in 1070 William ordered that the castle and the nearby St Mary's Chapel should be rebuilt in stone.

The castle was held by the Counts of Eu during the Norman period. King John ordered that the castles at Hastings and Pevensey should be slighted in 1216 and Henry III refortified the castle in 1220. In 1287 severe storms lashed the south coast, and some of the cliffs fell at Hastings and took parts of the castle with it. Over the next 100 years the castle was left to erode and more of it fell into the sea. By the sixteenth century all that remained were badly overgrown ruins. Even then it was not left alone, and it suffered bomb damage during enemy air raids on Hastings during the Second World War. In 1949 the Hastings Corporation bought the three-and-a-half-acre site, stabilised the ruins and created ornamental gardens.

For many years Hastings was known to have two female ghosts. One was a 'woman in brown' who haunted the East Hill at Ecclesbourne Glen and the other was a 'woman in white', who wandered the ruins of

Hastings Castle on West Hill. All that seemed to be known of the ghostly woman in white, according to the local oral tradition handed down over the years, was she was named Agnes and she was an unmarried mother who had either been 'put to death' or committed suicide 'hundreds of years ago'.

In 1953 a photograph taken by a visitor was given to Hastings Castle guide Mr F. G. Green that had been taken in the castle grounds during a recent holiday. The snapshot was meant to be of a friend but when it was developed, it showed the figure of a woman who appeared to be holding a baby in her arms. Mr Green passed the image on to his manager, but he had not taken down any contact details for the woman who took the photo. Major William Dyer, the Hastings publicity director had the image checked by photography experts who assured him it was not a double exposure and did not appear to have been manipulated in any way.

An appeal to trace the woman who took the photograph reached the national newspapers. The *Daily News* featured the story in January 1954 and quoted Mr Stephen Isles (76), who had been custodian of the castle for twenty-five years who said he had 'lost count of the times' the ghost had appeared before him and his wife. Mr Isles described the spectre as 'A tall figure in white, she would come to us in the dungeons, glide silently down a passage. circle us and then disappear again'. He added, 'In the castle grounds I dug up the centuries-old bones of a child.'[10]

The story of the photograph drew a lot of publicity and in April 1954 a seance was held in the castle dungeons. Strict precautions to avoid publicity were taken until after the event when a *Hastings Observer* reporter was informed of what had occurred:

> The principals in the seance were a well-known London medium named Mrs Frank Brown, who was accompanied by Mr Fred Archer, editor of *Psychic Magazine*, Mr Leslie Howard, his assistant, and two other London journalists.
>
> The seance in the gloomy dungeons lasted two hours, and among those present were Mr Stephen Isles, who was for 25 years custodian of the Castle [and] Mrs Isles, both of whom claim to have seen the ghost many times, Mr W. H. Dyer. Director of Publicity, and Mr John Burton,

> Director of Entertainments. The Observer reporter was told that the medium went into trance and that her spirit guide, speaking through her. claimed to be in touch with a nun of the Order of St Agnes, who died in mysterious circumstance in 1080, not many years after the Norman Conquest
>
> The legend goes that the nun had a baby by a man who was either an important officer of the Castle or the Church. It is believed she was either put to death or committed suicide in shame for breaking her vows. The ghostly nun is said to carry a baby in her arms, but the medium said she was not carrying a child but that her hands were folded across her breast. She was wearing a light grey habit with the skirt falling in folds. This description tallied with the figure which Mr and Mrs Isles said they had seen flitting about the Castle grounds.
>
> Since the tragedy so long ago, the story says that the ghosts of the nun and the man who betrayed her have haunted the dungeons and the Castle grounds, and the medium said that both were 'trying to get back into the earth plane so that they could perform penance for their sin'.[11]

After the seance several photographs were taken in the grounds of the Castle in the hope of capturing another ghostly figure. Nothing was reported to say anything paranormal had been captured on any of the photos. The ghost of the woman in white is still occasionally seen among the ruins of Hastings Castle.

Herstmonceux Castle, Herstmonceux near Hailsham, East Sussex

Ever since the author bought his first books on British ghosts as a boy in the early1980s, purely on looks alone, Herstmonceux Castle established itself in his mind as the epitome of a haunted castle. It is a truly magnificent, moated castle built of Flemish bricks in 1440 by Sir Roger de Fiennes. It was famed for having a window for every day of the year and a chimney for every Sunday. In an article about Herstmonceux Castle published in *The Queen* in 1940 it was described as 'said to be haunted by horrible apparitions', the precise nature of which has never been determined, adding:

> Certainly, this castle has had a history which would warrant the presence of any ghost. Grace Naylor, a young and beautiful heiress, was starved to death in the Lady's Bower by her jealous governess. One of the owners was executed for murder at Tyburn. Three occupants died here raving mad.[12]

According to tradition, the castle was haunted by a phantom drummer who stood 9 feet tall and whose drums emitted blue sparks on every beat. He kept the countryside around the castle in a state of alarm with his nightly tattoo and by straddling along the battlements at a furious rate. In the eighteenth-century local folk were often startled by the beating of a drum that appeared to proceed from the 'Drummer's Hall', a three-windowed room between the towers over the porter's lodge around midnight. According to Horace Walpole, this story inspired Addison's comedy, *The Drummer*.

Another tale tells of how one of the previous owners of the castle had become a recluse and a rumour begun to circulate that he had died. His wife was still young and beautiful and when a suitor came to seek the hand of 'the widow', the reclusive husband frightened them off by booming out 'ghostly' beats on the drum. The problem, for the 'ghostly' drummer came when his young wife turned the key on the door of his retreat and left him to starve to death. The last laugh was on her though when the drum was heard again long after her erstwhile husband had died.

Years later it was claimed that the drumming was the work of a gardener at the castle, who was in league with the notorious Hawkhurst gang of smugglers. They used the dungeons beneath the tower as a treasure house for unlawful spoil and made the drumming to strike fear into the hearts of the naïve and superstitious locals to ensure they stayed well away.

Perhaps it was all a ruse after all but there is a postscript, said to have been supplied by 'an authority on the history of Sussex', published in the *Hastings & St Leonards Advertiser* in October 1905:

> An iron chest was accidentally discovered in a recess leading to the attic of the castle in 1738 by one John Miller,

> a domestic, and young Lancaster, a son of the steward, then boys at play. They found the chest in the wall, with two large hammers affixed thereto. They removed it into the room, and on striking it the sound resembled that of a kettle drum. They ran to communicate the joyful tidings to others, and on their return the chest was gone, and it was never heard of again, though every possible endeavour was made to discover the thief. Report says that three persons rose suddenly from poverty to affluence, and every one of them died mad.[13]

Another haunting is said to be the spirit of a young girl who was starved to death in the castle shortly before her twenty-first birthday in 1727 to prevent her inheriting a fortune. The ghost of this poor emaciated girl is said to have been seen wandering beside the moat.

Hever Castle, Edenbridge, Kent

The original Hever Castle, consisting of a gatehouse and walled bailey surrounded by a moat, was built around 1270 and owned by James Fiennes, 1st Baron Saye and Sele. From 1462 to 1539 Hever Castle was owned by Geoffrey Boleyn who converted what had become a decrepit old castle into a manor with new dwellings with the walls. The Boleyns had also upgraded themselves. They were not nobility but were very successful merchants in London and desperately keen to obtain status, even changing their name from Bullen to the more ostentatious Boleyn that intimated something of nobility and continental courts.

Thomas Boleyn inherited Hever Castle in 1505 and lived there with his wife Elizabeth Howard, daughter of the powerful Duke of Norfolk. The couple had seven children, one of whom they called Anne. The Boleyns had estates at both Hever Castle and Blickling Hall in Norfolk, and the children were raised knowing and loving both properties. Anne was despatched to the court of Archduchess Margaret in the Netherlands in 1513 and completed her education in France.

The refined and beautiful young Anne returned to England in 1522 and secured a position at the court of King Henry VIII as maid of honour to the queen, Catherine of Aragon. Anne caught the eye of King

Henry, but she refused to become his mistress: it would be marriage and acknowledgement as his queen and nothing less for Anne. The Pope refused to annul Henry's marriage to Catherine. This was not going to stop Henry, who broke with the Roman Catholic Church and created a new Church of England with Henry as its head. He annulled his own marriage, sent his old wife away and married Anne Boleyn in 1533.

Anne gave birth to a fine daughter who grew to become Elizabeth I, but she was not the son Henry craved. After suffering several miscarriages and the stillbirth of a son, Henry had had enough of Anne. She had also become very unpopular both at court and among her subjects after she failed to produce a male heir to the throne. Opinion sunk even further after the death of Henry's first wife Catherine and a persistent rumour arose that she had been poisoned on the orders of Anne or Henry.

On 2 May 1536 Anne was arrested and taken to the Tower of London where she would be tried before a jury of twenty-seven peers on charges of adultery, incest and high treason. She was found guilty, condemned to death and was executed within the walls of the Tower on Friday 19 May 1536. On the morning she was to die, Anne sent for William Kingston, the Constable of the Tower; they conversed and she said to him:

> 'I hear I shall not die afore noon, and I am very sorry therefore, for I thought to be dead by this time and past my pain.' I told her it should be no pain, it was so little. And then she said, 'I heard say the executioner was very good, and I have a little neck,' and then put her hands about it, laughing heartily. I have seen many men and also women executed, and that they have been in great sorrow, and to my knowledge this lady has much joy in death.[14]

The ghost of Anne Boleyn is believed to haunt several locations including the Tower of London, her Norfolk home of Blickling Hall and Hever Castle. She is said to appear in the clothes she wore for her execution; they were recorded as a red petticoat under a loose, dark grey gown of damask trimmed in fur, with a mantle of ermine. Anne Boleyn's ghost at Hever Castle has been seen most frequently on Christmas Eve, her head is intact and her expression is said to appear sombre as she drifts silently over the picturesque bridge that spans the River Eden in the grounds.

Leeds Castle, Broomfield, Kent

The first stone-built Leeds Castle was constructed by Robert de Crevecoeur on islands in the River Len in 1119. It remained in his family until the thirteenth century when it was bought by Queen Eleanor of Castile, wife of King Edward I. Edward favoured Leeds Castle and poured money into improvements of its defences, a barbican spanning three islands was built, a gloriette was added with apartments for the king and queen and a lake was created around the castle.

When the castle came to Henry VIII in 1519, he carried out wholesale improvements for his first wife, Catherine of Aragon, to live there. During the Civil War it declared for Parliament and was used as both an arsenal and a prison but was never besieged. By the early 1800s the Wykeham Martins family had inherited the fortress and embarked on an extensive repair and the remodelling of the castle in a Tudor style, that was completed in 1823 and left the castle as we know it today.

Leeds Castle is famous for its black dog that appears as a dreaded omen that someone who lives within the walls of the castle is soon to die. It has been suggested this manifestation might have been conjured by Eleanor of Gloucester, mistress and then wife of Humphrey, Duke of Gloucester who was accused of witchcraft in 1441. Eleanor was escorted to Leeds Castle by Sir John Steward and Sir John Stanley on 11 August and remained there for two months while awaiting trial. During her time at Leeds Castle, Eleanor attempted to escape by feigning illness but failed to convince anyone.

It could well have been purely malicious or a politically motivated accusation, but Eleanor was known to have consulted astrologers to try to divine her future. One of those she consulted, a certain Roger Bolingbroke, accused Eleanor of being the instigator, claiming that she had ‘first stirrd himme’ to know ‘to what astate she sholde come’. If she did possess powers or could call upon those who practised magic who knows what could have manifested that still lingers around the castle in her attempts to escape.

When she was examined by a panel of bishops headed by the Archbishop of Canterbury, Eleanor denied most of the charges of witchcraft, heresy and treason. She did however confess to obtaining potions from Margery Jourdemayne, ‘the Witch of Eye’, claiming they were only to help her conceive.

Eleanor was found guilty of 'treasonable necromancy' and had to do public penance in London. This consisted of walking through the streets dressed only in her shift carrying a taper; she was forcibly divorced, sentenced to life imprisonment in royal castles and was given a pension of 100 marks a year. The others did not fare so well. Bolingbroke was hanged, drawn and quartered at Tyburn, and Margery Jourdemayne was burned *De heretico comburendo* at the stake in Smithfield Market on 27 October 1441.

Pevensey Castle, Pevensey, East Sussex

Pevensey Castle has a long history of documented hauntings. It was originally constructed in as a huge Roman shore fort in AD 290 and it has been claimed that the tramp of the feet of a large and orderly body of ghostly Roman legionaries has been heard, but never seen, to march by.

After the Norman conquest of 1066 a fortress was built within the ancient walls and was the scene of numerous sieges and actions over the years. The ghost said to haunt the castle is known as the 'Woman in White' but there seem to be two possible candidates for who she was. It is a tale of two Joans.

The most likely candidate is that the ghost is that of Lady Joan Pelham, the wife of Sir John Pelham who was Constable of Pevensey Castle. In 1399, when Sir John was away fighting elsewhere, the castle was besieged by supporters of Richard II. Lady Joan courageously stepped up to the mark and commanded the defence of the castle. Things did start to get fraught, and she wrote asking Sir John to return with reinforcements. This he did and ended the siege. The ghost of Lady Pelham is believed to be seen gliding along the top of the outer walls looking out across the Weald for the return of her husband.

The second and final candidate for the haunting is Queen Joan of Navarre (1368–1437), wife of Henry IV. Her personal confessor, Friar Randolph, went before Parliament in 1419 and made claims that Joan had 'plotted and schemed for the death and destruction of our said lord the King in the most evil and terrible manner imaginable'. In effect he had accused her of killing the king by witchcraft. Consequently, her fortune was confiscated, and she was imprisoned at Pevensey Castle, and later at Leeds Castle in Kent.

Fortunately, her stepson, Henry V, felt remorse for her fate and, curiously, her accuser Friar Randolph was found strangled or, according to another account, he died after a brawl with a warder in the Tower of London. The dowager queen was finally released from captivity in 1422, her fortune was restored to her, and she would live out the rest of her days with her own court at Nottingham Castle. So, perhaps Pevensey Castle could be haunted not by just one but by two 'women in white' who never manifest at the same time?

In one dramatic sighting in 1984 a group of teenagers had pitched their tent near the castle and enjoyed a summer evening together but as the dusk turned to darkness they saw someone walking along the south side of the castle. The figure looked quite solid and human, who they might have assumed was just someone wearing a white coat out walking their dog. The problem was the person they were watching appeared to be 'moving along as if floating'.

The kids grabbed a torch and set off to follow the figure and see if they could get a better look at it. They found they had to clamber over a fence and up the ruins where the figure had just glided across as if their passage was unimpeded. They kept the apparition in sight and watched it as it reached a large bush in the shadow of the castle walls where it promptly disappeared. By the time the intrepid teenagers reached the spot they had not seen any sign of the figure leave and no one or anything that could have been mistaken for the figure seemed to be around.[15]

Porchester Castle, Porchester, Hampshire

Porchester Castle is often missed out by other ghost books, but I think is a great castle to visit. A castle has stood on the site for well over 1,000 years. Situated at the north end of Portsmouth Harbour, it is redolent of the martial history that took place within its walls and has wonderful views across the Solent. Founded as a Roman shore fort, much of those ancient walls are still standing, along with a Noman keep and a church that were added in the twelfth century.

It was at Porchester Castle that Edward III stayed with his army before crossing to France where they fought and won the Battle of Crécy in 1346. Henry V and his army would set off from Portland Castle before his famous victory at Agincourt in 1415.

During the Napoleonic Wars the old castle was used as a prison for French prisoners of war, including some 2,000 African-Caribbean soldiers captured during the fighting at St Lucia. But before the Battle of Waterloo in 1815 the prisoners were gone, the castle was abandoned and it fell into decay. The site was passed into the care of English Heritage in 1984.

The site is claimed to be haunted by ghosts from different ages of Porchester Castle's history. Among them is the 'Woman in White' who is said to be seen to fall from the battlements. A 'tall and whitish, misty form has also been spotted around the castle. A woman dressed all in black has been spotted lingering and bending over near one of the graves in the churchyard within the castle walls. A phantom horse and rider thought to date from the time of the English Civil War has occasionally been seen in the courtyard and hooves have been heard trotting along the central path of the castle. A ghostly monk has been seen gliding along the outside of the castle wall near the church.

In the early twentieth century a woman visitor was crossing the keep to a breach in the west wall that allowed access to a spiral staircase when she encountered the ghost of a crusader knight kneeling on the stairs. In 1933 several newspapers reported the sighting of yet another ghost:

> The castle is at present under restoration by the Office of Works, and a tradesman who delivered goods at the castle declares that when leaving the grounds in his car in pitch darkness early in the morning, he was terrified by the sight of a white human figure standing in an angle of the castle walls. … The figure, he said, appeared to be watching him. Returning home at the end of the day he found that his business partner had had a very similar experience on leaving the castle an hour later. The new ghost is said to resemble a sentry.[16]

Rochester Castle, Rochester, Kent

The imposing and well-preserved stone keep of Rochester Castle has stood guard over the east bank of the River Medway and Watling Street (the London Road) since the twelfth century. The castle endured an epic siege by King John when it was a rebel barons' stronghold in 1215.

Despite undermining the outer wall and using the fat of forty pigs to fire a mine that brought the southern corner of the keep down, the defenders managed to hold out. But after two months their supplies were exhausted, no more could get through and they were starved into surrendering. The castle was besieged again during the Second Barons' War in 1264 and saw action for the last time in 1381 when it was captured and ransacked during the Peasants' Revolt.

The following story of the haunted at Rochester Castle comes from an old, yellowed cutting from the *Kent Messenger* of April 1935 that I found stuck on the page of a scrapbook many years ago. It comes from a time when newspaper reports on ghosts and hauntings could still be found that had a real element of storytelling which is seldom found today. I hope you will enjoy reading it (as I have) exactly as it was written all those years ago:

> Have you heard about the ghost of Rochester Castle? She ought to be floating around the southern battlements sometime next week-end with an arrow stuck in her breast, her flowing white garments stained with blood and her raven tresses streaming on the night wind. All in accordance with the very best traditions of the supernatural and of crumbling castles.
>
> Take a stroll round the castle walls one night next week-end and you may be rewarded by seeing the poor lady silhouetted in her long, white robes against the sky. Midnight would be about the best time. It was Mr George Bourner, who is retiring after 28 years as keeper of the castle and its grounds, who revealed to me that the Lady of Rochester Castle is supposed to have been seen in recent years 'But I've never seen her myself,' he added.
>
> Whose is this eerie spirit, and why ought it this Eastertide to be haunting the battlements of the romantic old pile that dominates Rochester and the Medway? I sought the answer from Mr Edwin Harris, who knows more about the castle, old houses, spooks and underground passages in Rochester than anyone else:
>
> 'At Easter in the year 1264,' said Mr, Harris, 'the rebel Simon de Montfort, arrived outside the walls of Rochester.

> He put the city to the sword, then laid siege to the castle, which was gallantly defended by Earl de Warrene. During the siege Gilbert de Clare, one of De Montfort's knights, conceived a plan to seize the beautiful Lady Blanche, daughter of the Earl. ... By a cunning ruse he gained entrance disguised in a suit of armour identical with that of Ralph de Capo, Lady Blanche's lover, and was already carrying her towards the wooden stairs when de Capo espied him from Rochester Bridge. Seizing bow and arrow from an archer, he shot at Gilbert. The arrow struck the knight's armour, glanced off it, and entered the bosom of the Lady Blanche. She fell dead on the spot and the same night her ghost walked on the battlements. And it is said, it continued to haunt them at midnight for a long time.'

Mr Harris reluctantly confessed he had never seen the ghost of Lady Blanche, despite having watched for her early and late at night on more than one occasion. But, as the article pointed out, 'people have sworn to him they have seen her'.

Charles Dickens (1812–70), the author of such classics as *A Christmas Carol*, *Oliver Twist* and *Nicholas Nickleby* loved Rochester. He had wanted to be buried in the Rochester Castle Moat Burial Ground but was honoured with a grave at Westminster Abbey instead. His ghost, however, is said to return and has been seen strolling around his desired burial site. He is most frequently seen around Christmastime when he has even been spotted setting his watch by the clock at the Rochester Corn Exchange around midnight on Christmas Eve.

Old Scotney Castle, Lamberhurst, near Tunbridge Wells, Kent

> Creeper-grown and the colour of lichen, standing with the grey and rust coloured barbicaned castle tower against a steep wilderness of quarry and flowers behind, and at its foot the lily moat reflecting sky, trees and ruined mansion, to-day it makes an exquisite picture. If ever ruin making had justified itself this has.

So wrote Rose Macaulay of Old Scotney Castle in *Pleasure of Ruins* (1953) and her words remain true today as the castle remains a picturesque ruin that provides a romantic backdrop for a pleasant afternoon stroll, but it does have a darker history.

The original Scotney Castle was built by Roger de Ashburnham in 1378. It passed to the Darrell family in 1418 and would remain in their hands for the next 350 years. The Darrells would build the stone fortified house with towers at each of its corners in the fourteenth century. By 1558 only the south tower was standing. In 1580 the south wing we still see today was rebuilt in the wonderful Elizabethan architecture style, and around 1630 the eastern range was rebuilt in three storeys in the style of Inigo Jones. In 1720 George Darell made further alterations, capping the Ashburnham Tower with its distinctive conical tiled roof and glazed cupola.

In 1778 old family disputes and debts of the Darrells finally led to the castle being sold to Edward Hussey. His grandson, also named Edward, built the 'new' castle to the designs of Anthony Salvin and abandoned the old castle to become a picturesque ruin. In 1863 Hussey bought the neighbouring early Georgian manor house of Finchcocks at Goudhurst from Richard Springett. Mrs Springett was known to have had a stern attitude toward any who had a belief in the paranormal. Apparently, a footman claimed he had seen a ghost, but Mrs S was having none of it; she flatly refused to have any of her servants seeing ghosts and threatened that the next member of her staff to report seeing one would face instant dismissal and no more was heard of it. It is a good thing the deal was not reversed, and it was not her husband who was buying Scotney Castle as she may well have seen a ghost herself!

Scotney Castle is reportedly haunted by a few ghosts. The spectre of a beautiful young woman has been seen near the castle keep and the figure of a man dressed in eighteenth-century garb has been spotted in the rock garden above the quarry. Probably the most infamous ghost also dates to the eighteenth century when the property was in the hands of Arthur Darrell who had a highly lucrative sideline in smuggling. When he was abroad, the news arrived at Scotney that he had died, and that his body would be transported back to the castle for burial.

A goodly number of mourners gathered for the funeral on 12 December 1720 but among them stood a mysterious, tall, cloaked figure, his face muffled against the cold with a scarf. As the coffin was solemnly lowered into the grave the tall stranger said in hushed tones, 'That is not me!' and vanished. A fine postscript to this story is provided by John Bailey, the sexton of Lamberhurst Church who died in 1867. He claimed when he was preparing a grave in the 'Scotney Chapel' in the church he came upon an unmarked, studded coffin. Hoping to find some clue as to identity of who lay within, he prised off the lid only to discover it was filled with stones …

It seems that Arthur Darrell did not only need to disappear to avoid the revenue men; it was rumoured he had murdered one of them, either by drowning him in the moat or had dumped his body in it. Either way he needed to disappear to escape the hangman. It was not long afterwards the ghost of a revenue officer was said to have been seen to rise from the moat, dripping with the stagnant water and stalks the house knocking on the door and trying to gain admission. To end up in the moat was particularly horrible when you consider it was into that same moat that the castle toilets and drains discharged their waste and it would not just be lilies that adhered to the body of the murdered revenue man.

Windsor Castle, Berkshire

Windsor Castle is the oldest and largest occupied castle in the world. Founded by William the Conqueror in the eleventh century the castle has stood for nearly 1,000 years, has been the home of forty kings and queens and has been rebuilt and expanded many times.

Many ghosts are said to linger in the castle and its grounds; the figure of twenty-five different manifestations is often stated, and they include some of the monarchs who lived there. Among the most frequently reported are the groans, wheezing and the sound of Henry VIII dragging his ulcerated leg said to be heard in the Cloisters. Unlike King Henry who tends to be heard rather than seen, the ghost of King Charles I has been spotted in the Canon's House and is said to have been seen so clearly that he was easily recognised from his portraits.

The ghost of Queen Elizabeth I has appeared at a window in Dean's Cloister and is known to haunt the Royal Library. Her Majesty has been seen, and the heels of her shoes have been heard clicking along on bare floorboards and across the library into an inner room on several occasions. One of the best attested sightings of the queen's spectre was made by Lieutenant Arthur St Leger Glyn, 3rd Battalion, Grenadier Guards in the library in 1897 and the account of what he saw was widely published in national and local newspapers:

> An apparition has been seen in Windsor Castle. An officer of the Grenadier Guards, Lieutenant A. St Leger Glyn, 3rd Battalion Grenadier Guards, was favoured with the sight. That something strange had undoubtedly been seen is vouched for upon high authority. The Bishop of Peterborough, for instance, told several people about an uncanny appearance, and the bishop's nephew, Lieutenant Glyn, was mentioned as one who was prepared to vouch for a strange occurrence. So a representative of the 'Daily Mail' set out to find the truth.
>
> After a long search the mother of Lieutenant Glyn, the Hon. Mrs Sidney Glyn. was found, and this lady astonished the enquiring newspaper man by remarking quietly, in reply to the question introducing this eerie topic that there was truth in the matter.
>
> From the communication the lady then proceeded to make it appear that this Royal phantom is no mere conventional spirit. The Hon. Mrs Carr Glyn said: – 'It is perfectly true that my son has witnessed something abnormal. He was, he tells me, sitting in the library of Windsor Castle reading a book, the 'History of Dorsetshire', to be exact. As he read, he became aware of somebody passing in the inner library. He looked up and saw a female figure in black, with black lace on the head, falling on to the shoulders. The figure passed across the library towards a corner which was out of view as my son sat, and he did not take much notice, thinking it was somebody reading in the inner room.
>
> 'This was just upon four in the afternoon, and an attendant soon afterwards came up to close the place. My son asked who was at work in the inner room, and the attendant replied that no one else was in the library.
>
> 'My son assured the attendant that a lady had just before walked across the inner room. "Then where could she be?" asked the attendant, having ascertained that nobody was

in the inner room. "She must have gone out of a door in the corner," said my son, indicating the corner to which the figure had passed. "But there is no door," said the attendant.

'My son said nothing about this incident, and did not think very much about it, I understand, until Mr Holmes, the librarian, asked him about it, the attendant having mentioned the matter to Mr Holmes. Asked by Mr Holmes to describe the figure he had seen, my son did so, and Mr Holmes replied that my son had seen the apparition of Queen Elizabeth. Mr Holmes added that there were records that this apparition haunted these rooms, but Lieutenant Glyn was the first man in our time who had seen it. The Dean of Windsor also asked my son about it, and several members of the Royal family have interviewed him on the subject.'

The Hon. Sydney Carr Glyn, the famous Crimean veteran, and father of Lieutenant Glyn, upon learning of the topic under discussion, said: 'If my son says he has seen anything, you may take it from us that he has seen it.' Both the Hon. and Mrs Carr Glyn gave permission for the publication of this statement by their son, subject to the sanction of Lieutenant Glyn. On Sunday night a wire was despatched to Lieutenant Glyn, soliciting leave to give the story on his authority, and yesterday morning came the answer, 'Certainly, if you like. – Glyn, Grenadiers, Islay.'

Mr R. R. Holmes, the librarian of the Castle, conducted the interviewer to the scene of the alleged apparition, and said that this gallery has had the reputation of being haunted by the ghost of Queen Elizabeth from time out of memory. His own recollection of the story dates from twenty-seven years ago, and he has been in the habit of spending Halloween in the gallery for several years in the hope of encountering her deceased Majesty. He had heard some rumour to the effect that the Empress Frederick had, when a child, seen an apparition in the gallery.[17]

Lieutenant Glyn had no reason to make the incident up, nor did he ever seek publicity from it. He went on serve in the South African War and with distinction during the First World War, where he was mentioned in despatches and retired a lieutenant-colonel. Early on during the Second World War Princess Elizabeth (later Queen Elizabeth II) and her sister Princess Margaret are believed to have seen the ghost of Elizabeth I in the library, as did their father King George VI.

The ghost of King George III has been seen looking out of a window of a room just below the library, as he did in life, watching his soldiers at drill on the parade ground. A newspaper article in circulation in 1959 claimed rooms where George III had been confined during his bouts of madness had remained unoccupied and locked since his death in 1820. The article goes on to state, 'servants dislike going to that part of the royal residence lest they hear him ceaselessly muttering behind the locked doors as some are said to have done.'[18]

The terraces outside the castle are also where phantoms are known to walk as Guardsman Bentley found out to his cost in 1906. Here is the account of the incident and its consequences as published in *Dundee Evening Telegraph* on 6 March under the headline of 'Windsor Castle Ghost: Apparition with "Piercing Eyes" – Sentry Shot Through It':

> One of the ghostly apparitions domiciled at Windsor Castle is suffering from a fit of restlessness. Its most recent exploit was discussed yesterday at a military inquiry held upon a private of the 2nd Coldstream Guards, who was doing sentry-go along the historic East Terrace on Saturday [3 March 1906].
>
> Five shots ringing out in the early morning in the direction of the King's and Queen's apartments, overlooking the East Terrace, caused the guard to turn out with feverish haste. It was found that the sentry had fired the whole of the contents of his ammunition pouch at a ghost – which he thought he saw gliding up the steps of the terrace towards the castle.
>
> 'I challenged it,' says the private, 'and it made no reply, so I filled my rifle with ball cartridge and let go. The thing came to a standstill only a few yards from me, but apparently the first shot made no impression, so I reloaded, and fired straight at it. The bullets must have gone clean through the ghost, but they left it unharmed, for I fired the whole my five rounds, and then it disappeared.'

> When his comrade on sentry-go at the other end the terrace heard the shots, he hurried up and found the man who had seen the ghost in a dazed, affrighted condition. 'I have seen a ghost and shot the beauty,' he was told. The second sentry looked in the direction pointed out by his fellow-soldier but could see nothing of a ghostly nature. The moonlight lit up the sombre wall of the castle; the fountain bubbled as it played in the beautiful sunken garden, but beyond this everything was as still as a churchyard at midnight. The second sentry said he could see nothing uncanny. 'It must have cleared off,' replied his scared companion.
>
> By this time the castle guard had turned out and the first guardsman having repeated his story to the officer in command, the terrace was searched in all directions; but there was no trace of any ghost, and the conclusion of the unavailing hunt was the arrest of the sentry, who has been confined since Saturday, and was brought before the authorities yesterday.
>
> The private – whose name is Bentley – appeared before Major Lambton at the Victoria Barracks. He was accused of firing without proper cause but stoutly defended his action. 'I gave the challenge – Halt! Who goes there?' he said, 'and, receiving no answer, had to use my rifle.' The upshot of the inquiry, however, was that Bentley was sentenced to three days' confinement to the barracks. Naturally unsympathetic people are saying that the sentry must have suffered an hallucination; but the guardsman adheres his story, and, besides, he is not the first man to see ghost at Windsor Castle.[19]

The article concluded: 'There are a lot of statues on the East Terrace. and the frightened guardsman may, of course, have been aiming at one these.' You can almost hear the cogwheels of military authorities whirring away to produce a 'rational explanation' that will kill the ghost story and lo! and behold! The following appeared in the press shortly afterwards:

> It is now suggested that what excited his [Guardsman Bentley's] imagination was one of the stone elephants

> brought from Lucknow, which stand on pedestals on either side of the stone steps leading from the gardens to the terrace of the castle. One of these figures bears several bullet marks. In mitigation of the soldiers action, it may be stated that in the moonlight the elephants have a somewhat uncanny appearance.[20]

Tragedy stuck on the on the South Terrace overlooking the Long Walk at Windsor Castle on Wednesday 22 June 1927 when Guardsman Leon Cedric Skiller of No. 2 Company, 2nd Battalion, Grenadier Guards committed suicide while on sentry duty by shooting himself in the head. Guardsman Skiller had been acting out of character of late, and had confided to Guardsman Walter Moss, that he 'was not right in the head'. Before going on guard on the morning of the tragedy, he had told Guardsman Reid that it would be for the last time because 'he was going to do himself in'. Reid, however, had not taken him seriously.

A few weeks later another Guardsman was on sentry duty in the same area and decided to make one last patrol of the Long Walk before he was due to be relieved. Having completed the outward length, as he turned to march back, he saw another guardsman walking towards him. As the figure drew closer, he could clearly make out the features of the smiling face of Guardsman Skiller, his comrade who had committed suicide on that very spot. The spectre of the smiling guardsman has continued to be seen on the terrace over the years

Windsor Great Park is said to be haunted by a ghost known as Herne the Hunter. The origins of this manifestation may well be a deity of a far earlier date. The story attributed to the haunting has several different versions but in essence they tell the same tale. Herne is said to have been a keeper in the royal forest on the staff of King Richard II. When the king was out hunting, he injured but did not kill a stag with one of his arrows. The incensed animal charged at the king, Herne threw himself in front of the stag and slew it with his dagger, saving the life of the king but was fatally gored in doing so.

As Herne lay on the forest floor, his life blood ebbing away, a stranger (a wizard or the Devil in disguise, depending on the story) strode out from the trees and informed the king if he wished Herne to be saved the horns of the stag that killed him should be cut off and bound to his head. This was done and by this magic Herne was restored to life. Over the weeks after the incident Herne's fellow woodsmen became increasingly jealous of the favouritism the king showed him. In other versions of the story Herne committed or was blamed for some misdemeanour. Whatever the cause, Herne was let go by the king. The following day he was found hanging from a great oak tree and stories of the tree, the forest and Great Park being haunted by Herne arose soon afterwards. He even gets a mention in Shakespeare's *Merry Wives of Windsor* (1597):

> *There is an old tale goes that Herne the Hunter*
> *Sometime a keeper here in Windsor Forest*
> *Doth all the winter-time at still midnight*
> *Walk round about an oak with great ragged hornes;*
> *And there he blasts the tree, and takes the cattle*
> *And makes milch kine yield blood and shakes a chain*
> *In a most hideous and dreadful manner.*

The tree known as Herne's Oak was believed to have been felled in 1796. It was then claimed the tree that had been cut down was not the actual tree and the 'true' Herne's Oak was still standing. Sadly, this mighty oak was blown down in the great storm of 1863. Other oaks have been planted since and carry on the name. Herne's ghost is said to appear when the royal family face turbulent times or England is in danger.

Herne has been seen on several occasions by people from all walks of life over the years, and some of the kings, queens and nobles at Windsor have seen him. Newspapers in the early twentieth century recorded:

> At midnight if the weather was favourable, some would wrap up and go out into Windsor Great Park to listen for the bugle horn sound by the legendary Herne, and it is actually said that on the eve of the Crimean conflict December, 1853, and again in 1856 before the Mutiny, these curious echoes were heard, and the dash of hunters' steeds as well disturbed the quiet. There are people living at Windsor who swore last year trouble was coming to England, for that on the Christmas night of 1898 Herne was out.[21]

Herne was reportedly seen shortly before the outbreak of war in 1914 and during the years of the conflict. When the author's great-grandfather was in a military encampment at Windsor Great Park for a short while when serving in the Norfolk Regiment during the First World War, there was talk of Herne being seen by one of his comrades on sentry duty. They did not know the story of Herne and the young soldier had been startled to see the figure of a man 'with antlers growing out of the top of his head' standing in the moonlight. He appeared quite solid, his features could be discerned, and the sentry was sure it was not a stag that had wandered up. The figure he saw was a man, he was sure of it, but he was 'there one minute and gone the next' before the sentry could issue a challenge. The sentry reported the matter to his sergeant wondering if someone was 'larking about.' Enquiries were made but all men in the camp were accounted for.

The ghost of Herne has also made other appearances over the years, sometimes on his own, sometimes followed by a wild hunt. Notably, he was reportedly seen in 1926 around the time of the General Strike, before the abdication of Edward VIII in 1936 and before the death of George VI in 1952, and sightings are still being reported up to very recent times.

Chapter 7

The South West

She is, probably, the most ominous and dangerous ghost in England.

Weekly Telegraph

Berkeley Castle, Berkeley, Gloucestershire

The first castle at Berkeley was built shortly after the Norman conquest as a motte and bailey, by William FitzOsbern around 1067. The castle passed to the original Berkeley family in the twelfth century and then to Robert Fitzharding and his wife who became the founders of the Berkeley family who still own the castle.

The deposed King Edward II was confined in Berkeley Castle in 1327. While there he died. Parliament was told that the king had suffered a fatal accident, but rumours abounded that he had been murdered. Some suggested the king was suffocated whereas others have described an even more horrible end devised so no mark of violence would be immediately apparent on the king's body. Raphael Holinshed's *Chronicles* recorded:

> they [the murderers] came suddenlie one night into the chamber where he laie in bed fast asleepe, and with heavie featherbeds or a table (as some [sources] write) being cast upon him, they kept him down and withall put into his fundament [his anus] an horne, and through the same they thrust up into his bodie an hot spit, or through the pipe of a

> trumpet a plumbers instrument of iron made verie hot, the which passing up into his intrailes, and being rolled to and fro, burnt the same, but so as no appearance of any wound or hurt outwardlie might be once perceived. His crie did moove manie within the castell and towne of Berkley to compassion, plainelie hearing him utter a wailefull noise, as the tormentors were about to murther him, so that diverse [others within the castle] being awakened therewith (as they themselves confessed) praied heartilie to God to receive his soule, when they understood by his crie what the matter ment.[1]

It would be Thomas de Berkeley who escorted the body of the dead king to Gloucester Abbey for burial; he would later be charged with being complicit in the killing of the monarch. Berkeley swore the murder had been carried out by agents of Roger Mortimer, the queen's lover, while he was away from the castle. Mortimer was condemned without trial and hanged at Tyburn in 1330. Berkeley was fortunate to be believed and was cleared of all charges in 1337.

The cell where Edward is supposed to have been imprisoned and murdered can still be seen at Berkeley Castle. The horrific agonies he suffered as he was murdered are echoed in the blood-curdling phantom screams said to be heard in and around the castle on 21 September, the anniversary of his death, every year.

Berry Pomeroy Castle, Berry Pomeroy near Totnes, South Devon

One of the first hauntings that I read about that really chilled me as a youngster with an interest in ghosts was the story of Berry Pomeroy Castle. Even after all these years it can truly be said the stories of the hauntings still make me shiver and when you visit the place it really does have a very dark atmosphere about it; I know I am not alone in this feeling.

The ruins of Berry Pomeroy castle that we see today consist of a Tudor mansion built within the walls of a fifteenth-century castle by the Pomeroy family who had held the land since the eleventh century.

The Pomeroys got into financial difficulties in the sixteenth century, and Sir Thomas Pomeroy sold the property to Edward Seymour, 1st Duke of Somerset (Protector Somerset) in 1547, whose son, also named Edward, made it his home. Berry Pomeroy Castle was abandoned in the late seventeenth century when the fourth baronet moved to Wiltshire. The Reverend John Prince, vicar of Berry Pomeroy, described the property as it was in the 1690s in his *Worthies of Devon*, I am particularly drawn to his closing remarks:

> The apartments within were very splendid, especially the dining-room which was adorned, besides paint, with statues and figures cut in alabaster with admirable art and labour; but the chimney-piece of polished marble, curiously engraven, was of great cost and value. Many other of the rooms were well adorned with mouldings and fretwork; some of whose marble clavils [carved adornments] were so delicately fine that they would reflect an object true and lively from a great distance. In short the number of the apartments of the whole may be collected hence; if report be true, that it was a good day's work for a servant but to open and shut the casements belonging to them. Notwithstanding which 'tis now demolished and all this glory lieth in the dust buried in its own ruines, there being nothing standing but a few broken walls which seem to mourn their own funeral.[2]

Even those who know nothing of Berry Pomeroy Castle's ghosts but love visiting historic sites, and are very down to earth, often describe the place as 'eerie' and speak of feeling 'uncomfortable' there. Berry Pomeroy Castle ranks among the most notorious haunted ruins in Britain. Even back in the 1930s and 1940s articles on the ghosts of the castle did not mince their words:

> Everyone, probably, has heard the Berry Pomeroy ghost, believed to be the spirit of the very lovely daughter of a certain Lord of Pomeroy, and to be earthbound for certain unpardonable sins. She is, probably, the most ominous and dangerous ghost in England. When she wrings her pretty

> slender hands or appears very grief-stricken it is sure sign someone associated with the castle will die shortly.[3]

Other articles told of:

> The shadowy ivy clad ruins of Berry Pomeroy Castle, in South Devon, are enclosed in a deep wood, which superstition says is the haunt of a hundred evil spirits. God fearing men shun the woods of Berry Pomeroy when night has fallen. ... From the beginning tragedy beset the castle. A Pomeroy murdered his sister and her betrothed because the lover was from a hated family. Father and son, mother and daughter fought one another over the family gold and during one of these fights the whole family rushed over a precipice in the ground and perished.[4]

Among the ‘unpardonable sins’ committed within the walls of Berry Pomeroy Castle, are claimed to have been those of Eleanor de Pomeroy who is said to have imprisoned her younger sister Margaret and to have left her to starve death, for no other reason than they both fell in love with the same man.

Margaret is supposed to have died in a dark and dank dungeon that was at the bottom of a winding stone staircase, beneath the fifteenth-century bastion known as St (or Lady) Margaret’s Tower (located at the extreme right-hand end of the wall from the gatehouse). Margaret’s ghost is said to roam the depths under the tower and many visitors have claimed to have felt her presence in the stairway leading to her former cell. On certain nights of the year, especially around Christmastime, her beautiful ghost is said to leave its sepulchral dungeon and walk along the ramparts in long flowing white robes, beckoning to those who see her. Those who succumb to her coquettish smile and womanly allure and attempt join her fall to their death or grave injury.

Darkest of all is the story of the ghost known as the ‘Blue Lady’, named so because her ghost appears to wear a blue cloak. She is said to have been a Pomeroy daughter who was made pregnant by her own father. When the baby was born, she is said to have either smothered or strangled it and consequently her ghost is doomed to wander the castle in painful remorse for evermore. The crying and screaming of the baby are said to have been heard echoing around the ruins on many occasions.

An often-repeated story of the sighting of the 'Blue Lady' appeared in various newspapers and books over the years; here is a good version published in 1899:

> The remarkable story of the apparition at Berry Pomeroy Castle, near Totnes, appears to be authentic, and is well known in the West of England. The legend runs that in the latter part of the last century Dr Walter Farquhar, who was then at Torquay, was called to the Castle to attend the steward's wife. On his arrival he was shown into a room on the ground floor and asked to wait a moment. After some minutes had elapsed he grew impatient and arose to question a female who had opened a side door and was walking across the room. … His surprise, however, was great when he noticed her manner and garb. She was dressed in rich attire, but in an absolutely out-of-date costume, and wrung her hands in a pitiful manner – her face evincing signs of great distress.[5]

Dr Farquhar would vividly recall visage of the woman in his memoirs:

> If ever human face exhibited agony and remorse; if ever eye, that index of the soul, portrayed anguish uncheered by hope. And suffering without interval; if ever features betrayed that within the wearer's bosom there dwelt a hell, those features and that being were then present to me.

The published account continued:

> She walked to the flight of oak stairs and, quickening her pace, disappeared. At that moment the steward entered the room and announced that his wife was ready to see him. Dr Farquhar found his patient dangerously ill, and he was so much engrossed with the case that he forgot to question

> the steward as to the young lady in the curious dress he had seen.
>
> On the following day he found his patient much improved and remembered to ask the steward about the mysterious young lady. As the Doctor recounted his experience the poor fellow showed unmistakable signs of fear and trembling, and told the Doctor that now he was sure his wife would soon die, as the spectre was the spirit of the daughter of an early owner of the Castle who had murdered her child, and had since appeared as an omen foretelling the death of a castle resident. Dr Farquhar quickly gave the steward every assurance of his wife's turn for the better, and that he thought she would continue to improve, but the credulous old steward would not hear of it. The next day the Doctor called at the Castle and was astounded to find that his patient had died soon after he left the place the previous evening The most strange part of the story is to come.
>
> After an interval of several years, Dr Farquhar was well known in London as Sir Walter Farquhar (1796) and could count among his clients and friends certain members of nobility and Royalty. One day a lady came to him in great distress, saying her sister was ill, and appeared to be wasting away, and that on being questioned, she was most emphatic in saying she saw a ghost when visiting in Devonshire some weeks before, which had left such an impression upon her, that do what she would she could not shake it off. The lady further said that the spectre appeared at Berry Pomeroy Castle, at which Sir Walter started, told her of his experiences, and requested to see the young lady immediately, whom he found suffering as described. The poor girl appeared greatly relieved to be speaking to some one who shared her uncomfortable experience, and, it may be added, her sister soon regained her usual health.[6]

All were relieved the ghost had not claimed the sister, but then, like the good doctor she had only been visiting when she saw the apparition.

However, they learned soon after, that the old steward of Berry Pomeroy Castle had finally passed away.

Cadbury Castle, Cadbury, Somerset

I have always loved the legends of King Arthur, the knights of the round table and the quest for the Holy Grail. There are a few hauntings associated with the story too, notably the ghost of Merlin the wizard that is said to haunt Merlin's Cave at Tintagel. Indeed, the whole site has a feeling of mysticism and an ancient magical past older than the ruins that still stand above the cave is palpable.

A similar feeling can be experienced at Cadbury Castle, an Iron Age hillfort and earthworks said to have been the real Camelot, where legend tells of how Arthur and his knights sleep below until they are summoned again when the country is in dire need. A door in the hillside is said to open every seven years so Arthur and his knights can leave to feed their horses.

There is another tale that a ghostly King Arthur and his knights ride out each Midsummer's Eve along an old trackway between Cadbury and Glastonbury known as 'King Arthur's Hunting Causeway'. The journal of the *Somerset Archaeological and Natural History Society* noted in 1890:

> In the neighbourhood of Cadbury Castle, one of the reputed sites of the Arthurian Camelot, we find 'King Arthur's Hunting Causeway'. There seems to be no road or lane there, but that would be no handicap for ghostly horsemen, and sometimes on rough winter's nights King Arthur and his hounds are heard along this track. And folks do say that on the night of the full moon King Arthur and his men ride round the hill, and their horses are shod with silver, and a silver shoe has been found in the track where they do ride: and when they have ridden round the hill they stop to water their horses at the Wishing Well. Not content with all this, King Arthur and his knights come riding down from Camelot to drink the waters of a spring beside Sutton Montis Church on the eve of every Christmas-day.[7]

In his excellent book *Haunted Castles* (1974) Marc Alexander recounts how on a Midsummer's Eve shortly before the First World War a local woman who did not live far from Cadbury Castle was driving home with a friend and they saw 'a string of lights moving down the great mound, and as she drove nearer these turned out to be flames illuminating the points of lances carried by a troop of mounted warriors, led by a tall man of majestic bearing'.[8] The knights on their mounts advanced silently without even the sound of hooves, jangle of reins or clank of armour, and they vanished as mysteriously as they appeared.

Corfe Castle, Corfe, Dorset

Corfe Castle was built by William the Conqueror on a commanding hill on the route between Wareham and Swanage. After undergoing major structural redevelopment in the twelfth and thirteenth centuries this fortress was sold by Elizabeth I to Sir Christopher Hatton. Corfe Castle was sold on again in 1635 to the Lord Chief Justice, Sir John Bankes. When Civil War broke out, it declared for King Charles I. In May 1643 Sir John was away fighting when a detachment of Parliamentarian troops came to seize the cannon at the castle. Lady Mary, her six daughters and a force of just five men sent the Roundheads on their way.

Lady Bankes petitioned for reinforcements and another eighty troops were despatched to the castle. The Roundheads, however, also returned in larger numbers in June with a force of over 500 armed troops and two siege engines but they were denied.

Corfe was one of the last remaining Royalist strongholds in southern England. Lady Mary and her own small party held the Upper Ward as the troops fought from other strategic areas around the castle parts of the fortification. The defenders held out remarkably well until 26 February 1645 when they were betrayed from within by Colonel Pitman who discreetly opened the sally gate and allowed the Parliamentarian troops to rush in. The castle fell soon afterwards but Lady Bankes and her daughters were given safe passage and, in an unprecedented mark of respect, she was permitted to take the keys of the castle with her. In 1646 Parliament ordered Corfe Castle be slighted, barrels of gunpower were brought in and it was blown up, leaving the ruins seen today.

For years afterwards 'ghost lights' have been seen on the steep hill around Corfe Castle. Some claim they are the ghosts of the Roundheads killed in the fighting for the castle. It seems the smugglers capitalised on the story and used it to their advantage to keep superstitious locals away as they carried out their nocturnal activities in the area, but the lights have been seen since those times. During the Second World War the local Air Raid Precautions workers and Home Guard were led a merry dance around the castle mount on more than one occasion when lights were seen on the castle mound during the blackout. Reports of the lights have not appeared so often over more recent years but in the 1970s Marc Alexander mentioned in his book *Haunted Castles* (1974) that his friends in Dorset had informed him 'phantom figures' were sometimes seen among the castle's ruins 'as evening darkens the sky'.

There have also been reports of the ghost of a headless 'white lady' who stands silently amid the ruins of the castle whose presence is said to send shivers down the spine of anyone in her presence. (If I found myself in the presence of the headless spectre, I think I would have shivers down my spine too.) She then fades away. The headless ghost of the 'White Lady' has even been seen near the road leading to the main gateway on several occasions including notable sightings in the 1960s and 1970s. On one night in 1967 John Seager was driving along the road and thought the figure ahead of him was a woman in a white nightgown but as he drove closer, he had to suddenly slam on the brakes:

> It was a white figure, headless, that drifted across the road in front of me. It moved down the path at the foot of castle hill, near the bakery. I suddenly found myself trembling with coldness … it was an experience I would never want again.[9]

Who the spirit was and why she appears to have been decapitated remains a mystery.

Dunster Castle, Dunster, Somerset

Dunster is a castle that just resonates history. The first known castle on the site was constructed just after the Norman Conquest in the eleventh century by William de Mohun and was replaced with a stone keep in the twelfth century; it withstood a siege during the early years of The Anarchy. In the late fourteenth century, the Mohuns sold the castle to the Luttrell family, and it remained in their family until the late twentieth century.

The history hidden behind some of the walls is undoubtedly dark. During restoration work in the gatehouse the skeleton of a man who had stood over 6 feet tall was found in chains with his wrists and ankles still in fetters. The remains had been there centuries but surely if he had died in the shackles they would have been removed before he was entombed … or were his captors keen to ensure he stayed put even after his death?

One story that has passed into legend at Dunster Castle dates to the English Civil War, when Dunster Castle's garrison was under the command of Colonel Francis Wyndham; it withstood siege by Parliamentary troops for 160 days. At one point the Roundhead commander, Colonel Robert Blake, abducted Colonel Wyndham's mother and threatened to stand her in front of the line of fire unless Wyndham surrendered the castle. As Blake issued the challenge Wyndham's mother urged her son to 'do your duty'. The muskets may have been ready to fire but Colonel Blake backed down. Dunster Castle was only surrendered when the Royalist cause was lost in 1646.

Perhaps it is Colonel Wyndham's mother who returns and wanders the castle as the ghost known as the 'Grey Lady' dressed in seventeenth-century clothes; she frightened generations of the Luttrell children with her appearances, usually during thunderstorms.

A ghostly Roundhead also puts in an occasional appearance in the Leather Room at the Gatehouse. He has been seen by both visitors and staff and just disappears through a closed and solid wooden door. Dunster Castle is a National Trust property and if you have not been before I think it is well worth a visit. The sense of history felt within its walls suggests there are many more spirits there than I have mentioned.

Okehampton Castle, Okehampton, Devon

Okehampton Castle consisted of a motte and bailey on high ground commanding a crossing point of the West Okement River, built between 1068 and 1086 by Baldwin FitzGilbert. It has been a ruin for many years, and one ghost story is linked to it. It related a certain 'Lady Howard', who, according to legend, murdered three of her husbands and two of her children. It is possible 'Lady Howard' was based on the real Mary Fitz (1596–1671), the daughter of Sir John Fitz of Tiverton and Lady Bridget Courtenay of Powderham. Three of her husbands all died; after the death of the third, Sir Charles Howard (hence 'Lady Howard'), she married Sir Richard Grenville whom she divorced amid much scandal.

The ghost of Lady Howard was said to travel every night in a spectral carriage made from the bones of her dead husbands, accompanied by a ghostly skeletal hound from Okehampton Castle to Launceston Castle. In another version the carriage hurtles silently along from Tavistock to Okehampton. Lady Howard is doomed to repeat the journey, said to convey a single blade of grass from start point to destination until the end of time. No matter the route, it was said if you were out and about the headless driver would always be willing to pull up to collect or even snatch up passengers and kill them along the way. An old traditional Devon rhyme recounted:

My Ladye hath a sable coach
And horses two and four.
My Ladye hath a gaunt blood-hound
That runneth on before.

My Ladye's Coach hath nodding plumes,
The driver hath no head.
My Ladye is an ashen white,
As one that long is dead.

'Now pray step in,' my ladye saith,
'Now pray step in and ride.'
I thank thee, I had rather walk
Than gather by thy side.

The wheels go round without a sound
Or tramp or turn of wheels;
As cloud at night, in pale moonlight,
Along the carriage steals …

I'd rather walk a hundred miles
And run by night and day
Than have the carriage halt for me
And hear the ladye say – 'Now pray step in, and make no din,
Step in with me and ride; There's room I trow, by me for you,
And all the world beside.

Old Wardour Castle, Wardour, Tisbury, Wiltshire

Old Wardour Castle is an impressive ruin of a six-sided tower house of a unique design in England that was built by Baron Lovell in the 1390s. The Lovells supported the Lancastrian cause during the Wars of the Roses, and after all was lost the castle was confiscated from them in 1461. It then passed through several hands until it was purchased by Sir Thomas Arundell in 1544.

In the English Civil War, the castle was Royalist and was besieged by Parliamentary forces on 2 May 1643. With her husband away the defence of the castle fell to Lady Blanche Arundell who held out for nine days against a Roundhead force said to number over 1,300 men and artillery under command of Sir Edward Hungerford and Colonel Edmund Ludlow – an achievement made more remarkable because she did so with only her children, a few maid servants and twenty-five men. Lady Blanche surrendered on what had been agreed as honourable terms, but the terms were not honoured, the castle was sacked, and she was removed as a prisoner to Dorchester. The ghost of the betrayed Lady Blanche, still dressed for battle, is said to appear occasionally around dusk at Old Wardour Castle.

Pengersick Castle, Praa Sands, Breage, Cornwall

Pengersick Castle is a fortified manor built around 1510 by William Worth that passed to the Milton family who enlarged it later in the sixteenth century. There has been many events in that castle that may have caused hauntings over the years. In his introduction to *The Ghosts,*

Hauntings, Myths and Legends of Pengersick Castle, Ghost Club member Robert Snow wrote:

> Pengersick Castle is a building of great antiquity and had long had a reputation of being associated with sorcery, witchcraft, black magic and murder. Throughout its history it has been considered an evil place, somewhere to be avoided, especially during the hours of darkness.

The castle is believed to be haunted by the ghosts of Henry Pengersick (aka le Fort) (1267–1329) and his wife Engrina Godolphin (1271–1357), a monk and a nurse. An investigation of the hauntings was carried out over three nights by members of the Ghost Club in 1997. The team was led by Trevor Kenward armed with tape recorders and SLR cameras loaded with high-speed photographic film (just think of the tech used by many paranormal investigators today). It was reported most of the activity they witnessed and recorded at the castle had taken place from around midnight and then faded as the time passed until it was almost all over by 3.30 a.m. (the classic chime hours). During that time, they witnessed not just a murder but a double murder from 600 years earlier replayed by the ghosts in the castle.

They reportedly witnessed several spectral scenes from which they believed they were able to piece together the story of how Henry Pengersick murdered a monk who he caught in the act of attacking and attempting to rape his wife. The wife was attended by a nurse, she collapsed onto the bed in the room, where she appeared to have died too. The members of the club who witnessed the apparitions described them as sometimes appearing looking quite transparent, other times they appeared quite solid when they appeared in 'The Haunted Bedroom' on the third floor. Mr Kenward commented: 'Sometimes you might stand at the door to this room and not want to open it because of the 'feeling of something evil inside … the atmosphere in the bedroom has been full of emotion and very unpleasant, almost evil'.[10]

What really happened all those years ago I am not sure we will ever find out for sure but sightings of a ghostly monk wearing a wide-brimmed hat, near the medieval garden and a woman, writhing in agony after appearing to have been poisoned in the haunted bedroom have been seen. There have also been reports of mischievous, ghostly children, a phantom cat and a huge black devil dog – although the spectral dog might have been the creation of local smugglers to frighten away any curious locals when they were about their business under the cloak of darkness,

Powderham Castle, Powderham, Devon

Powderham Castle was built by Sir Philip Courtenay around 1400 on the flat ground on the west bank of the estuary of the River Exe where it is joined by its tributary the River Kenn. It has been the seat of the earls of Devon for centuries.

A revenant known as the 'Grey Lady' is said to haunt the castle and has frequently been seen in the library. The spirit is said to be that of Lady Frances Courtenay, formerly Lady Frances Finch (1720–61), wife of William Courtenay, 1st Viscount Courtenay. Although her appearance is not terrifying her presence is accompanied by a sudden drop in temperature and to witness her appearance is believed to be an ill omen that a death would soon occur in the castle household.

The other ghost is a young woman who appears outside the castle with a baby in her arms. She is thought to be the unquiet spirit of the woman and a baby who had been found hidden behind a wall in the Guard Tower during renovations in the early nineteenth century. The bodies were given a decent burial in nearby Powderham Church but the woman's spirit continues to haunt the locality. The ghost made a dramatic appearance in February 1939, and a *Western Morning News* reporter went ghost hunting, his report stating:

> A few days ago, an Exeter man claimed to have seen a shrouded figure of a woman standing in the roadway, near Powderham Church, and thinking it was a stranded pedestrian, stopped his car. 'To my amazement.' he said, 'the figure simply vanished. I got out of my car and looked all round, but there was not the slightest sign of anybody.' Later by the churchyard he claimed to have seen the figure slip through the churchyard gate. Armed with torches and accompanied by two friends, our representative kept a vigil for an hour in the vicinity of the church.

> However, whether the alleged ghost funked a battery of torches and preferred to remain in its spectral home or not, the apparition did not present itself. High hedges silhouetted in a full moon lined the road where the ghost was stated to have been seen first. Here there was nothing but an occasional rustling of leaves to disturb the silence of the night. Girls in the village are treating the story as somewhat of a joke, but most of them carry torches and walking sticks.[11]

Mr George Godbeer (born 1875), a villager who had lived at Powderham all his life, was asked by the reporter, 'Do you really think a ghost was seen?' He replied:

> Well, I would not say no. About twenty years ago I was walking with the then rector of Powderham on some ground beside the Castle. I was under the impression my wife and daughter were out of doors, and when I saw two figures in front of me, I naturally thought it was them. I said nothing to the rector, but on nearing my house saw by the burning lights that my wife and daughter were home and looked again. The figures I had mistaken for my family had simply disappeared. I asked the rector, and he said he too had seen them. We could not understand it. Three weeks later my daughter died suddenly and was buried in Powderham Cemetery.[12]

Sherborne Castle, Sherborne, Dorset

Sherborne Castle was originally constructed in the twelfth century as a fortified palace for Roger de Caen, Bishop of Salisbury and Chancellor of England. It had a turbulent early history; during the Anarchy in the 1140s the castle was considered 'the master key of the whole kingdom'.

Sir Walter Raleigh (1553–1618), the explorer, soldier and statesman credited with introducing potatoes and tobacco to Britain from the new world, fell in love with Sherborne Castle, and being in favour with Queen Elizabeth I she leased the estate to him in 1592. Raleigh built the lovely Sherborne Lodge nearby so that he could enjoy the view of the old castle ruins. The antiquary John Aubrey described it as 'a delicate Lodge in the park, of Brick, not big, but very convenient for its bignes, a place to retire from the Court in summertime, and to contemplate'. And this Raleigh surely did.

One wonderful story, how true it is I cannot attest to, but it has been handed down the years. Raleigh was relaxing under one of the trees on the estate enjoying his pipe. At that time the smoking of tobacco was still quite a new thing and a servant bringing Sir Walter a pitcher of ale thought his master's beard to be on fire and promptly sought to extinguish it by tipping the contents of the pitcher over him. Fortunately, Sir Walter saw the funny side of it.

The ghost of Sir Walter Raleigh has been seen many times walking the grounds dressed in the fine clothes he wore when attending court. He is said to stroll among the oaks until he reaches his favourite stone chair, where he pauses to gaze out across the estate he loved. His ghost is said to become particularly active around the anniversary of his execution on 29 September.

Today, the ghost of Lady Charlotte Digby haunts the house in the Blue Drawing Room, the Green Room and the short corridor that links them and has been seen by staff and visitors alike. If Lady Charlotte is not seen it is believed she is the cause of the strange feeling occasionally experienced by visitors in the corridor and the rustle of her ladyship's dress has been heard in the Green Room.

Footsteps have also been heard hurrying along the upper floors when there is no one there but it is Sir Walter Raleigh's bedroom where there is the feeling of another presence in the room and even being watched has been regularly experienced by staff in the empty house as they shut the house and lock down for the night. Two notable experiences were recorded in the *Memoirs of Georgiana, Lady Chatterton (1806–1876)* published in 1880:

> I could scarcely have been four years old, when we were staying at Sherborne Castle, an old place belonging to Lord Digby, in Dorsetshire. It was built by Sir Walter Raleigh, and is situated on a height, overlooking a large piece of water with the fine old ruins of an older castle on the opposite bank. The castle was so full on our arrival that my

old Scotch nurse and I were put into a large room, which, as I afterwards heard, was said to be the haunted room; nobody would sleep in it, and strange noises were heard at night to come from it. My nurse did not know of this at the time, nor did my mother. My impression is that I was much pleased to find myself in this large room; for it was in the third story, and the views from its windows over the beautiful terrace garden, which sloped down to the water, and the ruined castle beyond, enchanted me.

I slept in a little cot which had been placed close to a large old fashioned bed of carved oak with red velvet curtains, where my nurse slept. In the middle of the night, I was awoke by a brilliant light that shone upon the wall. As I looked wonderingly at it, figures of men fighting seemed to pass over it, like the reflections produced by a magic lantern. Groups of figures passed to and fro, shouting as they advanced and retreated. The colours were very vivid. I saw red coats and black, and flashing of fire arms, and heard horrible noises. I was very much frightened and looked round to my nurse for help. She was sitting up in bed, and to my still greater horror I saw she was not awake, but her eyes were fixed, though she seemed to be making signs to the figures, talking to them and motioning them to go away, while they were yelling and quarrelling.

I could neither cry out nor move – I was so frightened but continued to look at the strange appearance. Suddenly it vanished, and all was dark and silent. A feeling of horror and dread, which I still feel when I happen to think of it, kept me awake until the day dawned through the window curtains, when I went to sleep. I never mentioned this horrible scene to my nurse, nor to anyone else, till many years afterwards, when I told her about it, and asked if she had any recollection of it. She answered that she had not.

We often stayed at Sherborne Castle afterwards, but I never heard of anyone else being put in that room to sleep. It was directly over the one my mother generally had, and one night she was awoke by a violent knocking overhead. She described it as of dead bodies falling, or being thrown

> about, on the floor overhead. My father heard it too, and as there was a little turret staircase that wound up to the floor above out of their room, he determined to go and see what it could be. He lighted a candle and ascended the narrow winding staircase. He found the door of this large mysterious room open, but no one was in it. He had the courage (as I afterwards thought) to pass through the room, and went out at the other door, which opened on the great staircase, and came down again to my mother. The strange noises had ceased, and they never heard them again.[13]

Sudeley Castle, Sudeley, Gloucestershire

Sudeley Castle was founded in 1443 by Ralph Boteler, the Lord High Treasurer of England. It was later seized by the Crown and became the property of King Edward IV and passed to King Richard III, who built its magnificent banqueting hall. It then came to Katherine Parr after the death of her husband Henry VIII, and it would be her final home.

The castle has many ghosts; some just seem to appear briefly and fade away; even well-loved family pets have been thought to linger in spirit form. The ghost of a tall lady in a green dress has been seen on several occasions in the castle nursery. Her appearances are often presaged by a gentle waft of apple-scented perfume.

One member of staff did not seem to want to leave too. Janet Green came to Sudeley Castle from Inverness to be a housemaid in 1895 and worked there for fifty years, retiring as housekeeper; she ensured everything in the house ran like clockwork and ruled below stairs with a rod of iron. She kept a particularly keen eye on the young housemaids, many of them young unsophisticated girls from South Wales who were away from home for the first time, to ensure their maintained high moral standards and even stood watch at the top of the stairs to ensure no men on the staff tried to visit the maids after dark. Even after her retirement Janet would return to the castle and if things were not up to her exacting standards, she would still berate staff as if she had never left. Janet died in the 1950s but her ghost is still seen busying herself around the house and she has even been known to shake her duster at visitors who stray away from tour groups.

The ghost that has been seen over the greatest span of years is Queen Katherine Parr. After the death of Henry VIII, she married Thomas Seymour; at last, she had married a man of her own choice and for love. She was 36 years old and soon fell pregnant for the first time. She gave birth to her baby, Mary, on 30 August 1548, but Katherine fell ill with puerperal fever and died on the 5 September (her baby Mary is believed to have died about age 2).

Katherine was buried in the chapel of St Mary at Sudeley but over the next two centuries, her original tomb was 'mutilated and defaced', and the location of her burial place was lost until it was rediscovered in 1782. It was identified by the lead plate on the coffin lid that read: 'K. P. Here lyeth Quene Kateryne wife to Kyng Henry the VIII and Last the Wife of Thomas Lord of Sudeley ... dyed 5 September.' *A Brief Historical Account of the Castle and Manor of Sudeley* recorded:

> the curiosity of some ladies who happened to be at the castle in May 1782, to examine the ruined chapel and observing a large block of alabaster fixed in the north wall of the chapel, they imagined it might be the back of a monument formerly placed there. Led by this hint they opened the ground not far from the wall and not much more than a foot from the surface they found a leaden envelope, which they opened in two places, on the face and the breast, and found it to contain a human body wrapped in cere-cloth. ... Upon removing what covered the face, they discovered the features, and particularly the eyes in perfect preservation. Alarmed at the sight, and with the smell, which came principally from the cere-cloth they ordered the ground to be thrown in immediately without judiciously closing up the cere-cloth and lead which covered up the face, only observing enough of the inscription to convince them it was the body of Queen Katherine.[14]

In May 1784 another group opened the grave and found that 'air, rain and dirt having come to the face it was entirely destroyed'.

In October 1786 Katherine's grave was opened again with the Honourable John Sommers Cocks, John Skipp of Ledbury and another gentleman obtaining permission to examine the grave from Lord Rivers. They found:

> the face totally decayed, the bones only remaining; the teeth, which were sound, had fallen out of their sockets. The body, I believe is perfect, as it has never been opened; we thought it indelicate and indecent to uncover it but observing the left hand to lie at a small distance from the body we took off the cere-cloth and found the hand and nails perfect, but of a brownish colour.

Even then she was not allowed to rest and worse happened, Okell's account continuing:

> At the commencement of the year 1792 the remains of the Queen were again exhumed by a set of bacchanalians, when outrages so disgraceful were perpetrated, that a veil must be drawn over them.

In 1817 the grave was opened yet again but nothing remained in the coffin 'but a confused heap of bones, and a small portion of the hair, adhering to fragments of the cere-cloth under the skull. The hair, which was remarkably silky, and in colour a very bright auburn appeared as strong as when the body was first interred'.

The remains of Queen Katherine were removed from the ruined chapel to the adjoining chapel in a good state of repair and were placed in a stone vault near the remains of George, 6th Lord Chandos in the hope she could now rest unmolested. It does not seem like all those who desecrated the last resting place and remains of the Queen got away with suffering any consequences. Local farmer John Lucas was one of them, and the story is he went mad, swearing he had seen her ghost standing by her grave.

In 1860, in a well-documented incident, estate worker Fred Simmons had been asked by the chatelaine of the castle, Mrs Emma Dent, to repair broken a blind in the castle. He came in the evening and worked by candlelight; when he finished, he was leaving through the Chandos Room when his candle suddenly blew out. He then felt a woman rush past and he distinctly heard her silk dress rustling. He presumed it to be Mrs Dent but on speaking to the castle housekeeper, Mrs Bayliss, he was assured that he had been alone upstairs at the time. Mr Simmons would later confess that he had taken a tooth from Katherine Parr's coffin. Writing in his notebook, he pondered:

> Could it be so, that the ghost of Katherine was permitted to roam over those old precincts – making night hideous – and to fill with awe those who had been guilty of robbing the dead!

Mrs Simmons urged her husband to return the tooth to the coffin.

The remains of Queen Katherine have rested under a handsome tomb designed by Sir Gilbert Scott in 1859 but after all that disturbance and desecration it is no wonder her ghost still walks the corridors of Sudeley Castle.

Taunton Castle, Taunton, Somerset

Taunton Castle began as a fortified episcopal residence that belonged to the bishops of Winchester. Between 1107 and 1129 Bishop William Giffard converted the property into a motte castle with 13-feet-thick walls, inner and outer baileys and two 15-feet-deep moats with gatehouses and drawbridges. The castle has been used as a military base, prison and court where the Assizes and Quarter Sessions were held until 1858.

During the Civil War Taunton was one of the staunchest Parliamentarian towns in England and the castle was besieged three times. The fiercest fighting took place in 1645 when the town and castle were bombarded by Royalist forces, but Taunton never fell, a victory remembered in the town on 11 May as 'the day the Cavaliers ran away'. When Charles II was restored to the throne, his retribution was swift and he ordered that Taunton be destroyed and much destruction was carried out. The castle seen today has been added to and heavily reconstructed over the years, especially after Sir Benjamin Hammet, MP for Taunton, acquired the castle in 1786. He carried out extensive alterations in the Gothic style, the walls were refaced with chert, pointed-arched windows were installed in the curtain walls, and the great hall was reordered.

The 'Bloody Assizes' of 1685 presided over by the infamous Judge Jeffreys were held in the Great Hall of Taunton Castle. The trials were of the ringleaders and supporters of James Scott, 1st Duke of Monmouth, the eldest illegitimate son of Charles II. The duke had attempted to rise and usurp the throne that had been assumed by his uncle James II. The so-called Monmouth Rebellion began when the Duke of Monmouth returned from Holland in June 1685. He mustered his troops, stormed and took Taunton where he was proclaimed king at the castle.

After a few skirmishes the rising was finally put down at the Battle of Sedgemoor and more than 500 rebels were brought before the Assizes at Taunton on 18 and 19 September. Many of the participants who were found guilty were transported to the West Indies, but some 144 rebels found guilty of treason were hanged, drawn and quartered and their remains displayed in prominent places as a warning to all.

Over the years ghostly figures of a seventeenth-century gentleman holding a pistol has been encountered on the stairs and a 'grey lady' also dressed in clothing of the same period has occasionally been seen silently drifting along the corridors of the castle. Poltergeist activity has frequently been reported around the building by staff and guests. Staff are particularly reluctant to enter the Somerset Room because of its eerie atmosphere: things being moved around by unseen hands, things going missing, strange noises, knocks, footsteps are heard and 'cold spots' where the temperature suddenly drops to become 'icy cold' are experienced. The strains of tunes played on a violin have also been heard within the walls when no musician was playing and the ghostly tramp of the feet of the Duke of Monmouth's untrained army have been heard to march right through the castle and fade into the distance.

Tiverton Castle, Tiverton, Devon

Tiverton Castle was built by Richard de Redvers in the twelfth century and was rebuilt and much enlarged in the thirteenth and fourteenth centuries after it passed to the Courtenay family who became the earls of Devon. The castle was a Royalist stronghold during the Civil War but was taken after a brief siege by Parliamentarian troops under

Sir Thomas Fairfax on 18 October 1645. A contemporary account by the seventeenth-century historian John Rushworth recorded:

> Wherein was taken Colonel Sir Gilbert Talbot, the governour. Major Sadler, major to Col. Talbot. 20. officers of note. 200. common souldiers. Foure peece of ordnance. 500. armes, with store of ammunition, provision, and treasure.

The castle was then slighted and later converted into the fortified country house we see today.

Tiverton Castle is haunted by the ghost of a 'white lady' said to be a young woman in her bridal finery. The story attached to the haunting can be found in several castles and stately homes around the country. It is possible that this tragedy could have happened in more than one location; it certainly is recorded in the tale of 'The Mistletoe Bough' first published in the poem *Ginevra* by Samuel Rogers in 1822. Rogers noted, 'The story is, I believe, founded on fact; though the time and the place are uncertain. Many old houses lay claim to it.'

The legend tells of a young bride who is playing hide and seek with the other wedding guests around the castle and decides to hide in a large wooden chest in one of the bedrooms. She drops the lid but does not realise it locks itself. She waits and she waits but no one can find her and the poor girl suffocates. The night goes on and she cannot be found. The game stops being fun and guests have the horrible feeling that she is no longer hiding but that she has run off, perhaps with some secret lover. Over the years the chest in the infrequently used bedroom sat there unopened, no one knew where the key was and when it was finally broken into, the long-dead bride in her rotted wedding dress was discovered.

Endnotes

Chapter 1

1. *Carlisle Patriot*, Tuesday 26 June 1866.
2. *Penrith Observer*, Tuesday 13 November 1883.
3. *Sheffield Evening Telegraph*, Friday 3 January 1902 and *Manchester Courier*, Saturday 4 January 1902.
4. *Newcastle Daily Chronicle*, Tuesday 2 May 1922.
5. Catherine Crowe, *Night Side of Nature* (Newby 1848).
6. *Evening News*, Monday 15 November 1920.
7. Jeremiah Sullivan, *Cumberland and Westmorland, Ancient and Modern* (Whittaker 1857).
8. Ibid.
9. *Whitehaven News*, 30 October 2011.
10. *Newcastle Courant*, Friday 20 February 1885.
11. *Lancashire Evening Post*, Thursday 1 October 1903
12. *Kendal Mercury*, Saturday 4 August 1860.

Chapter 2

1. *Sunday Sun*, Sunday 19 April 1936.
2. *Teesdale Mercury*, Wednesday 12 November 1878.
3. Ibid., December 1879.
4. *North Cumberland Reformer*, Saturday 28 September 1895.
5. M. A. Richardson, *The Local Historian's Table Book of Remarkable Occurrences, Historical Facts, Traditions, Legendary and*

Descriptive Ballads Connected with the Counties of Newcastle-upon-Tyne, Northumberland and Durham (Richardson 1841).
6. *Newcastle Journal*, Friday 8 December 1939.
7. Terence Whitaker, *Ghosts of Old England* (Hale 1987).
8. John H. Ingram, *The Haunted Homes and Family Traditions of Great Britain* (Gibbings 1897).
9. John Aubrey, *Miscellenies* (Castle 1696).
10. *Illustrated Berwick Journal*, Thursday 7 October 1926.
11. Ibid.
12. Ibid.
13. *The Scotsman*, Saturday 23 March 1935.
14. Ibid.
15. *The Field*, 1 January 1999.
16. *Newcastle Chronicle*, Saturday 16 December 1893.
17. *Herald of Wales*, Saturday 8 February 1890.
18. *Newcastle Courant*, Friday 7 October 1887.

Chapter 3

1. R. E. G Cole (ed.), *Lincolnshire Church Notes made by Gervase Holles 1634–1642* (Lincolnshire Record Society 1911).
2. *The Spiritualist*, Friday 11 February 1881.
3. *Wolverhampton Express*, Wednesday 19 April 1978.
4. Ibid. Thursday 20 July 1978.
5. *Birmingham News*, Thursday 29 May 1997.
6. *Lincolnshire Echo*, Thursday 7 October 1897.
7. *Coventry Herald*, Friday 26 February 1915
8. *The Daily News*, Monday 7 March 1921.
9. *Nottingham Journal*, Thursday 10 March 1921.
10. Ibid.
11. *Weekly Dispatch*, Sunday 14 September 1902.
12. *Northern Weekly Gazette*, Saturday 18 December 1926.
13. Ibid.
14. Francis Richard Charles Guy Greville, 5th Earl of Warwick, *Memories of Sixty Years* (Cassell 1917).
15. Ibid.

16. James Harvey Bloom, *Laying a Ghost* in *Notes and Queries* Twelfth Series Volume IV (Francis 1918).
17. *Nottingham Evening Post*, Saturday 16 October 1926.

Chapter 4

1. Morley Adams, *In the Footsteps of Borrow and Fitzgerald* (Jarrold 1914).
2. Mackenzie E. C. Walcott, *The East Coast of England* (Stanford 1861).
3. James Harvey Bloom, *Laying a Ghost* in *Notes and Queries* Twelfth Series Volume IV (Francis 1918).
4. *London Daily Chronicle*, Wednesday 6 September 1922.
5. *Bedfordshire Times*, Tuesday 15 January 1861.
6. William Angus Drogo Montagu (9th Duke of Manchester), *My Candid Recollections* (Grayson 1932).
7. Ibid.
8. Anthony Wood, *Athenae Oxonienses* (vol2) (Rivington *et al* 1813–30).
9. Ibid.

Chapter 5

1. *Ballymena Weekly Telegraph*, Saturday 25 February 1933.
2. *Daily Herald*, Tuesday 23 December 1930.

Chapter 6

1. *Whitstable Times and Herne Bay Herald*, Saturday 17 September 1949.
2. *Maidstone Telegraph*, Friday 4 January 1974.
3. Ibid.
4. *Kentish Express*, Friday 16 August 1974.
5. *Dover Express*, Friday 22 February 1935.
6. *Kentish Express*, Friday 26 December 1958.
7. *Folkestone, Hythe, Sandgate & Cheriton Herald*, Saturday 10 March 1945.

8. *Gloucester Citizen*, Wednesday 28 February 1945.
9. *Manchester Evening News*, 19 November 1904.
10. *Daily News*, Monday 25 January 1954.
11. *Hastings & St. Leonards Observer*, Saturday 17 April 1954.
12. *The Queen*, Wednesday 25 September 1940.
13. *Hastings & St. Leonards Observer*, Thursday 5 October 1905.
14. Quoted in Christopher Hibbert, *Tower of London: A History of England from the Norman Conquest* (Newsweek 1971).
15. *Eastbourne Herald*, Saturday 25 February 1995.
16. *Clifton and Redland Free Press*, 6 February 1930.
17. *Daily Gazette*, Wednesday 10 February 1897.
18. *Linlithgowshire Journal*, Friday 4 December 1959.
19. *Dundee Evening Telegraph*, 6 March 1906.
20. *Birmingham Mail*, Tuesday, 6 March 1906.
21. *Bournemouth Daily Echo*, Wednesday 19 December 1900.

Chapter 7

1. english.nsms.ox.ac.uk/holinshed/texts.php?text1=1587
2. John Prince, *Danmonii orientales illustres: or, The worthies of Devon* (Rees & Curtis 1810).
3. *Ballymena Weekly Telegraph*, Saturday 26 December 1936.
4. *Good Morning*, Sunday 9 January 1944.
5. *Public Opinion*, Friday 31 March 1899.
6. Ibid.
7. *Somerset Archaeological and Natural History Society*, Vol. 36. 1890.
8. Marc Alexander, *Haunted Castles* (Muller 1974),
9. Peter Underwood, *This Haunted Isle* (Brockhampton 1998).
10. *West Briton & Cornwall Advertiser,* Thursday 4 September 1997.
11. *Western Morning News* Monday 6 February 1939.
12. Ibid.
13. Edward Heneage Dering, *Memoirs of Georgiana, Lady Chatterton. With Passages from Her Diary* (Washbourne 1880).
14. J. Okell, *A Brief Historical Account of the Castle and Manor of Sudeley* (Okell 1844).

Bibliography

Adams, Morley, *In the Footsteps of Borrow and Fitzgerald* (Jarrold 1914).

Alexander, Marc, *Haunted Castles* (Muller 1974).

Aubrey, John, *Miscellanies* (Castle 1696).

Cole, R. E. G. (ed.), *Lincolnshire Church Notes Made by Gervase Holles 1634–1642* (Lincolnshire Record Society 1911)

Crowe, Catherine, *Night Side of Nature* (Newby 1848).

Coxe, Antony D. Hippisley, *Haunted Britain: A Guide to Supernatural Sites Frequented by Ghosts, Witches, Poltergeists and Other Mysteries* (London 1973).

Day, James Wentworth, *Here Are Ghosts & Witches* (Batsford 1954).

__________, *In Search of Ghosts* (Muller 1969).

Green, Andrew *Our Haunted Kingdom* (Wolfe 1973).

Greville, Francis, 5th Earl of Warwick and Brooke, *Memories of Sixty Years* (Cassell 1917).

Hallam, Jack, *Ghosts of London* (Wolfe 1975),

Harries, John, *The Ghost Hunter's Road Book* (London 1974).

Hibbert, Christopher *Tower of London: A History of England from the Norman Conquest* (Newsweek 1971).

Hole, Christina, *Haunted England* (Batsford 1940).

Ingram, John H., *The Haunted Homes & Family Traditions of Great Britain* (Gibbings 1897).

Macaulay, Rose, *Pleasure of Ruins* (Thames & Hudson 1953).

Maple, Eric, *Supernatural England* (Guild 1989).

Montagu, William Angus Drogo, 9th Duke of Manchester *My Candid Recollections* (Grayson 1932).

O'Donnell, Elliott, *Haunted Britain* (Rider 1956).

__________, *Ghosts of London* (Allan 1932).

Okell, J., *A Brief Historical Account of the Castle and Manor of Sudeley* (Okell 1844).

Prince, John, *Danmonii orientales illustres: or, The worthies of Devon* (Rees & Curtis 1810).

Richardson, M. A., *The Local Historian's Table Book of Remarkable Occurrences* (Richardson 1841).

Robbins, Rossell Hope, *The Encyclopaedia of Witchcraft & Demonology* (Feltham 1959).

Storey, Neil R., *A Ghosthunter's Guide to Norfolk* (Countryside 2007).

__________, *A Grim Almanac of Cambridgeshire* (Sutton 2009).

__________, *A Grim Almanac of Essex* (Sutton 2005).

__________, *A Grim Almanac of Lincolnshire* (The History Press 2011).

__________, *A Grim Almanac of Suffolk* (Sutton 2004).

__________, *London Crime, Death and Debauchery* (Sutton 2007).

__________, *Hanged at Norwich* (The History Press 2011).

Thurston Hopkins, Robert, *Ghosts over England* (Meridian 1953).

Underwood, Peter, *Gazetteer of British Ghosts* (Souvenir 1971).

__________, *Haunted Isle* (Harrap 1984).

__________, *Where the Ghosts Walk* (Souvenir 2013).

Walcott, Mackenzie E. C., *The East Coast of England* (Stanford 1861).

Westwood, Jennifer and Simpson, Jacqueline, *The Penguin Book of Ghosts: Haunted England* (Penguin 2008).

Whitaker, Terence, *Ghosts of Old England* (Robert Hale 1987).

Wood, Anthony, *Athenae Oxonienses* (vol. 2) (Rivington et al 1813–30).

Acknowledgements

I would like to record my thanks to the following for their help and encouragement with this book and my research in this field over the years: British Library, National Archives, English Heritage, National Trust, Historic England, Essex Record Office, Newcastle City Library Local Studies Library, Bamburgh Castle, Castle Rising, Chillingham Castle, Colchester Castle, Dover Castle, Framlingham Castle, Lincoln Castle, Rochester Castle, Tower of London, Norwich Castle Museum, Castle Hotel, Taunton, Dave Schrader, Stewart P. Evans, David Hepworth, Rob Clack, Delianne Forget, Michelle Bullivant, Liz Cormell, Neil Packer, Chloe Baker-Cooper, Kerry Freeman, Martin Faulks, my much-missed friend the late Andrew Selwyn-Crome, all the teams of paranormal investigators it has been my pleasure to work with over the years, my commissioning editor and all the editorial and design team at Pen & Sword and, last but by no means least, my heartfelt thanks to my ever-loving family.

Index